Praise for *Cry All You Want, Just Get It Done* and Antonia Roybal-Mack

"This is a helpful guide to anyone considering divorce. It can prepare you for the realities of the situation and help you make an informed choice.

—Amy Morin, author of 13 Things Mentally Strong People Don't Do

"*Cry All You Want, Just Get It Done* is just the right blend of laser-sharp professional advice, personal insight, and step-by-step guidance and coaching about how to get through all the stages of divorce. Antonia Roybal-Mack is a Super Hero (Shero) in her own right, with a refreshing mix of vulnerable when sharing her personal experience and Badass Lawyer. She is a force to be reckoned with and has a humorous yet "No BS" attitude, which is clear from the very first line. No matter where you are in the process of divorce, you will find answers, tools, and inspiration in these pages. Throughout this book, Roybal-Mack takes you under her wing, and even if you never meet her, you know that she's got your back."

—Tanio McCollum, women's advocate

"There are people in our lives to whom we listen with our ears perked, and for me, Antonia Roybal-Mack is such a person. In *Cry All You Want, Just Get It Done*, Antonia offers new perspectives, proven strategies on the topic of choosing to divorce or not, and what to do next in the best manner possible. This is a profound read. Antonia's authenticity and straightforward talk grips you from the start. Her voice as an author is as real as she is in person. Having experienced a divorce almost 25 years ago, I found myself wishing I had this book and the influence of Antonia then. Antonia writes with a refreshing, real, and sometimes blunt voice that is a welcome approach in the processing of a tumultuous subject. It is evident by her education, experience, and awards that Antonia knows her stuff. This book is a gift to the rest of the world of her knowledge, wisdom, and very big heart."

—Kelly Cannon, professional certified coach, speaker, educator

"Informative. Moving. Powerful. This book is raw and personal; it hits home. Written by someone who lives it day in and day out and who has seen many outcomes, *Cry All You Want, Just Get It Done* gives great perspective. The resources and checklists are very helpful. There were many times I had looked for a resource on what to expect in the divorce process and how to prepare (brace) myself from beginning to end, and this book is it! The examples and stories were interesting, had a touch of humor, and invoked serious reflections of various possibilities. I highly recommend it."

—*Esther Lovato, former client*

CHAPTER 1

Should I Stay or Should I Go?

Y
ou were in love, you were vulnerable, you gave your spouse the power to destroy you, and he or she is doing just that. Now they are just a stranger with all of your secrets.

Should you stay or should you go?

How long have you known, deep in your heart, that your marriage was not working? How long have thoughts about the marriage consumed your entire being and taken your mind hostage? How many nights have you secretly Googled questions on divorce while your spouse slept next to you? How many showers have been consumed with thoughts of your partnership or lack thereof?

It goes without saying that marriage is hard. Divorce is hard too. So how do you decide to stay or leave? In my thousand-plus divorce cases, I have never told a man or woman to leave the marriage. You alone walked down the aisle to the altar and you alone need to make the decision to leave.

LET GO OF THE DELUSION

There are two major decisions that you will make in your life, and some will make these decisions more than once. The first decision is *Who are you going to marry?* and the second is *When, if ever, is it time to end the marriage?* Each day, I see the agony that my clients are in when they are making the decision to end their marriage. For some, the decision has already been made for them. Regardless of the path that you choose, you will be forever changed.

The first step is to be clear and ask yourself these questions:

- Are you sad about losing the marriage that you have and the relationship you once had with your soulmate?
- Are you sad about losing the relationship that you thought you'd signed up for, that had so much potential to be a grand love story, but never actually came to be?
- Are you clear about what is good for you, but there are external forces deluding you into staying?

I often hear the phrases "we had everything" and "everyone on the street envied us." While going through the divorce process, be honest while answering the above questions. Don't delude yourself. My clients who struggle the most have lived under the delusion that their marriage was perfect and feel blindsided by the mention of divorce. Despite their spouse showing them who they really are over and over again, these clients choose to hang on to the mere glimpses of good still present in their spouse, making excuses for their behavior rather than seeing them for who they truly are. Not who they were on their wedding day or who they want them to be—but who they are right now.

MY CLIENTS WHO STRUGGLE THE MOST HAVE LIVED UNDER THE DELUSION THAT THEIR MARRIAGE WAS PERFECT AND FEEL BLINDSIDED BY THE MENTION OF DIVORCE.

Mr. Investment

In one case, I had a very wealthy, smart, somewhat-famous client. When she started going through her divorce, she couldn't believe that she had "given her life" to her spouse and that he had betrayed her by leaving. The betrayal was so intense that she could not see anything beyond the anger.

On every call with her, I was reminded that everything that they had was "hers" and that she'd worked for it all while Mr. Investment sat home and played Mr. Investment with her earnings. She always described how they would both attend exclusive film openings in the finest clothing, with the finest and rarest jewelry, and how much he loved the lifestyle. Over time, when her brand started to diminish, the money that came along with it started to dry up.

Turns out, Mr. Investment was not in fact very good at investing and had lost almost everything that they had built, including their beautiful ranch estate in Santa Fe, which was being sold as a foreclosure, a word she would never utter aloud. Just to stay afloat, they had moved to an apartment the size of their master bedroom.

Despite the fact that Mr. Investment had lost everything that my client had earned, she still continued feeling the sting of rejection when he left her, believing it was for her, not him, to decide if the marriage was over. "How could **he** leave **me**?" she continually asked me. How could he "steal" everything they ever owned? How were they on the cusp of bankruptcy while attending the most exclusive parties?

Is it possible that Mr. Investment might have loved the lifestyle more than he loved his wife? I listened and coached my client away from the delusion that her life was perfect. Not only was the story that she told herself about her marriage false, but believing it made her divorce far more difficult than it needed to be because she went through it attached to a fantasy. This client was not in love with her reality; she was in love with her illusion, and so was her spouse. Even the lifestyle was an illusion because they could not afford it to begin with.

When you let go of the delusion—what you thought you had—it's much easier to move beyond the divorce.

WHEN YOU LET GO OF THE DELUSION—WHAT YOU THOUGHT YOU HAD—IT'S MUCH EASIER TO MOVE BEYOND THE DIVORCE.

IT'S OKAY TO STAY

While we just walked through one example as to why you might want to go, there is no right or wrong answer to "should I stay or should I go?" A marriage "yes" is not the kind of "yes" that comes with your first tattoo or your first shot of whiskey. It's not a "do the deed and look the other way." "Yes," with eyes wide shut, will not buy you peace and may end in the question "Did I stay too long?"

If you decide that you want to stay, there is one thing you must do: Commit. You do not need to commit for forever, but you need to commit for right now, maybe even just for today, and do the same exercise each day to decide which is authentic for you. What feels right for you is just that: Right for you. In making this decision, set aside all of the demons on your shoulder; set aside all of the judgments from your mother and girlfriends that he is "such an asshole." That he will never be worthy of your brilliance. That he will never be who you need, deserve, or want him to be. Ask your sister, mother, and bestie if their crystal ball is so much clearer than yours that they can make these statements with certainty.

If staying is right for you—whatever your reasons are—then it is okay. Just be very clear that this is what you want. You are the one who will live with your spouse. In the quiet moments when he is his best self and you are yours, it is okay to say this is enough for you. I have seen more marriages work after the divorce process has started than I can count. Those marriages were stronger after taking the time to do a deep dive into what needed to change. Change is a must.

Advice with a Slice of Pie

This story is one example of how the end can be the beginning. One snowy evening, I got a call from one of my clients who was a state trooper. It was New Year's Day. He was going to stop by for leftover pie after my New Year's party. This was a man who seemed to have it all. He had those clean-cut military good looks, money, a nice house, and a stunning and smart wife. The boxes were all checked. He was one of the most confident clients I had ever worked with. But I knew there were cracks in his suit of armor, so I agreed to see a client on a holiday in my home.

When he arrived, I put on a pot of coffee and found some leftover holiday pie. We sat down to "catch up." I knew this was anything but a social visit. I knew there were crises looming under the surface. As we sat in front of the fire, the cracks in his armor started to show. He told me that he had been under unbearable stress. He was unsure of his commitment to his wife and wanted to move forward with his divorce. I knew this discussion pained him.

As I began my archaeological investigation into what was happening beneath the surface, I learned that he and his wife were less than kind to each other. I learned that in the past twenty-four hours he had had to perform CPR on a child the same age as his own, and that the child had died despite his efforts. I learned that he had watched a semi-truck run over a man, and that he'd been the first at a scene that had left his own sergeant in the hospital, fighting for his life. Among all of that insurmountable human pain, he also felt that his wife didn't really love him. This was clear by the fact that he would rather come have coffee and pie with his divorce lawyer than go home. I understood this dynamic all too clearly from my own relationship, because I'd often found escapes from what loomed at home.

As we continued talking, I asked him why he had married his wife. From his answer, I understood that she brought peace and calm to his chaotic world. She was loyal, and in all of his military deployments, he never worried about her cheating on him. She held a demeanor of calm in the storm. It was clear that he loved this woman. But it was also clear that his top human need was uncertainty and adventure. This made him a powerful soldier and served him well in fighting wars. However, his top human need was not serving him in his marriage. During our conversation, I also learned that his wife's top need was love, connection, and certainty. This didn't mean that their relationship was doomed. It meant that he needed to go meet his human needs within the marriage.

As we finished the pot of coffee and my own husband began to wonder when my client was going home, I recognized that deep down this man did not want a divorce. He just didn't know what he didn't know. I told him that I would have the papers drawn up and ready for him to review the following week, but that we would need to meet in person to go over them. When we met, I told him that it was clear to me that he did not want a divorce, but that his trauma was probably too deep even for counseling to save them at this point. I asked him the same question I ask other clients: "Are you willing to do anything and everything necessary to save this marriage, so long as it is legal?" He answered yes. I told him that I would set the papers aside until he had spoken to someone and asked his wife to do the same.

I referred them both to individual master neuro-linguistic programming coaches. I didn't hear back from him. A few months later, I received a cake and a thank-you card from both of them. They had each redefined what they wanted in the marriage and made the decision to move forward together. They had been married in a civil service before his first deployment. Now they invited me to their church wedding, and I gladly attended. This is a reminder that even if you want something different, it still might be right in front of you.

IF YOU STAY, MAKE SURE YOUR MONEY IS PROTECTED

If you decide to stay in the marriage, regardless of if you are the wage earner or the spouse that has taken care of the family, there are things you can do to protect yourself financially, and each one will require a lawyer.

The first is a postnuptial agreement. This is a contract between you and your spouse that will allow you to divide property while you are still married. If you are worried about losing your business or losing some asset, write out an agreement that addresses your fears. If you are worried that he will run off with his business, write up an agreement that addresses your concerns. These agreements help you know if you are staying because you love your spouse and you want to make the marriage work, or if you are staying because the financial risk of leaving is too high. This agreement will allow you to stay without the fear of the latter.

The second tool available is to do specific estate planning with a postnuptial agreement. This will allow you to create a joint and separate trust. You put the assets that you intend to share and grow together in the joint trust, and if you get divorced in the future, that trust is all that is available to divide. You each have a separate trust as well that will secure some items from your security and growth bucket for your future. This is also generally a good thing to do if you or your spouse has children from another relationship. This may be more tolerable than a postnuptial agreement because they are prepared by estate attorneys and not divorce attorneys.

Another option is legal separation of assets. Depending on your state, you can stay living with your spouse but legally separate all of your assets. This creates a financial end date for the marital property. After that date, everything you acquire will be considered yours and not subject to division if there is a divorce in the future. There are pros and cons to taking this avenue, so it is imperative that you talk to a lawyer first.

The final option is sole and separate deeds or agreements. If you want to make sure that certain assets are secured for you in the event of the dissolution of the marriage, you can title property now with a sole and separate deed. This gives the owner of that property sole possession in the event of divorce.

While some people decide to leave, others, of course, decide to stay. Both decisions are right.

Life after Divorce

Early in my career, I sat across from a client who was leaving a fifty-year marriage. She'd gotten married just out of high school and had stayed married, despite knowing that her spouse was a compulsive gambler and a cheater (an unhealthy man). He was into other men, and during the period of time in which they married, it was more culturally appropriate to marry a woman and have a male paramour than it was to be openly gay. At the time, I simply did not have the right tools to help her understand that this relationship was not healthy for her.

When I asked her why she had stayed so long, her response astounded me. "I didn't think that I could know anything different in my life. I was just waiting to die." This was the first time in my career that I heard about "waiting to die," but it was not the last.

Don't get me wrong, she was not suicidal. She had just given up on any possibility that happiness could exist for her. A few years after her divorce was finalized, I saw her at a casino. She was wearing a shiny blouse and matching designer bag, a far cry from the grandma sweater she wore when I first met her. She was glowing. As we caught up, she pointed to her gray-haired fellow at the blackjack table. Someone who enjoyed the game, but not addicted. He was well-kept and must have been a heartthrob in his younger years—definitely retired military. She said with a grin, "Can you believe he is five years younger than me?" They had met at physical therapy, where he cheered her on after her knee surgery. It was apparent that she was no longer waiting to die. Most importantly, she was happy. She had made the hard decision and found that, even at her age, there was life after divorce.

Only you know what is right for you. Only you have to live with the decision.

If you're thinking of staying, ask yourself these questions:

- What would you do for this person at the start of the relationship?
- If you answered "anything," is he/she still worth the "anything"?

If you do what you did in the beginning, there will be no end.

THERE ARE NO BAD ANSWERS, ONLY BAD QUESTIONS.

When going through the exercises in *Cry All You Want,* understand that there are no right or wrong answers as long as you ask the right questions. There is no value in bullshitting yourself. No one is watching. Let the delusions and wishful thinking go and get real answers for yourself.

THERE IS NO VALUE IN BULLSHITTING YOURSELF. NO ONE IS WATCHING.

The first and most obvious question is: *Do you want a divorce?*

Even if the decision has been made for you, and your spouse has already filed for divorce and maybe even moved on with a new relationship, it is important to answer this valuable question so that you can find the power in your own situation by taking control of the answers. This will allow you to determine, regardless of others' actions or input, what is best for you in your own life.

Read the question again: *Do you want a divorce?*

The question is not:

- Do you want your current pain to end?
- Do you need a change in your marriage?
- Are you happy?
- Do you need the cheating/addiction/gaslighting/domestic violence to stop?

- Does one or both of you need mental health treatment?
- Does his mother need to go fly a kite, and once and for all, mind her own business?
- Do you need peace?

These questions may be pressing on your mind, but they are not the "right" questions and can be considered "bad" questions to be asking now. The "good" question to ask right now is—I think you're getting it now—do YOU **WANT** a divorce? Do you want the legal end to your marriage?

Pause and think before answering. The name of an all-time bestseller is *Think and Grow Rich*—so in this process, take time to think.

The question is not about what is best for the kids, best for your spouse, best for your business, best for your finances, or best for your religious beliefs. It's what's best for YOU. This may be the first time that you are asking: What is best for me? Imagine for a moment that you are on a high mountaintop and you are the only one affected by your actions and decisions—only you. Now, what would your answer be? Write that down.

THE ANSWER IS THE ANSWER. PERIOD.

Whatever you decide, there is a path forward. Each path will take commitment. Each path will have ups and downs. If you focus on the big picture and you understand your purpose and intention, you will make the decision that is right for you. It is okay if you decide to stay. It is okay if you decide to go. Regardless of your decision, it might be time to get your legal house in order. Now, just because you decide to stay, that does not mean that the pain will end immediately and never happen again. It just means you're willing to do it again, if that time comes.

I advise my clients, and I'll share this advice with you, that at the end of this process, you will get one of two things. You will get the peace of mind that you are on your own and that this road is yours alone—or your spouse will step up and be the parent and partner that you need. Both outcomes are okay. So make this decision alone with eyes wide open, and start down the path, whichever you choose.

AT THE END OF THIS PROCESS, YOU WILL GET
ONE OF TWO THINGS. YOU WILL GET THE
PEACE OF MIND THAT YOU ARE ON YOUR
OWN AND THAT THIS ROAD IS YOURS ALONE—
OR YOUR SPOUSE WILL STEP UP AND BE THE
PARENT AND PARTNER THAT YOU NEED.

YES OR NO?

Sales books always give advice on how to get to "yes!" This is not a sales book, so it is okay for the answer to be "no," "maybe," or even "WTF?" It is perfectly acceptable to say, "I don't know," and then keep reading. Speaking of sales, studies show that when a woman negotiates to buy a car for her best friend, she will negotiate better terms than she would negotiate for herself.[1] As women, we give better advice when we are helping someone other than ourselves. So, if you need to play that game, if you need to pretend that you're talking to a best friend who is in the same situation as you to get to your answer, then let the games begin!

AS WOMEN, WE GIVE BETTER ADVICE
WHEN WE ARE HELPING SOMEONE
OTHER THAN OURSELVES.

When you are ready to honestly answer that question, set aside some time and find a quiet place without distractions to answer the questions in Worksheet #1.

1 https://www.pon.harvard.edu/daily/business-negotiations/women-and-negotiation-narrowing-the-gender-gap/

"The world breaks everyone and afterward many are strong at the broken places."

—ERNEST HEMINGWAY

CHAPTER 2

No One Is Rewarded for Suffering—What Can You Take?

There is no award for the woman who can suffer the longest. Not all fairytales have a happy ending, nor is your life a romantic comedy—you and your spouse may not in fact be the kissing couple at the end. If social media has fueled your self-deception of your relationship by keeping the illusion alive and the relationship thriving in filtered, duck-faced photos of you on vacation with a cocktail in your hand, you are not alone. We don't often share the truth, the reality, the darkness that is happening in the pit of our souls, especially not on social media. Sometimes we are the only one who knows. Sometimes the issues are hidden so deeply inside of us that we can't find them, not even for ourselves. For others, inner darkness and personal issues burst out in very public, dramatic ways.

ASSESS THE SIGNS

The truth about leaving a marriage is that it's hard. It's emotionally painful. It can be financially damaging and it can feel unbearable. This is why we often ignore sometimes very obvious signs that things are not working for us. When people tell you what they are, listen.

Hear No Evil, Speak No Evil, See No Evil

One of my clients came to me numerous times while considering a divorce. The first time we met, she told me that her husband was a good father, that things in the house really weren't that bad. But as we got into details, over time she learned that her husband was sexually abusing her son, even going so far as to bring the kid to sex parties that he was having with other men. She didn't know the extent of the abuse when it was happening, but she knew her husband was a creep.

Another one of my clients and her children thought nothing of ducking every time that they drove by her ex's house. Her husband had shot at them before, so they were trained to duck and be on high alert around him. My client thought this was normal. For her, it was.

Finally, I had a client who was upset about her husband's alcoholism. She was used to seeing him sneak alcohol into all sorts of events, including school events. It wasn't until he started giving her eight-year-old son alcohol that she decided to do something about it.

These women were ignoring HUGE signs that it was time to go or make a change. There is no judgment; we all do it.

What signs in your life are you ignoring?

What stories have you told yourself that are just stories?

These are hard questions to dive into—knowing that we've ignored some big things doesn't feel good—but know this: We ignored these things for a period of time in order to protect ourselves. Delusion is your brain's way of protecting you from the truth.[2] Write down your answers and ask yourself again what you would tell your best friend to do.

2 https://plato.stanford.edu/entries/self-deception/

WHAT IS LOVE?

If you are being mistreated, your spouse does not love you. That is not what love looks like. The sooner you accept a new definition of love that includes all the good you deserve, the sooner you can attain that. The reward in this entire process is that you get to create that definition for yourself. You get to define "self-love" first.

> IF YOU ARE BEING MISTREATED, YOUR SPOUSE DOES NOT LOVE YOU. THAT IS NOT WHAT LOVE LOOKS LIKE.

Several years ago, I moved out of my house with my children, leaving my husband alone. We moved into a much smaller house while I worked through some of these questions. Did I want to stay? Did I need to go? One thing that I realized during this period of time is that for me, love means having peace, which means being with someone who will do anything for me. At that time in my life, I also realized that I wasn't doing anything for myself, so I started working self-care into my schedule. I started exercising and making myself good, healthy lunches. For me, defining love meant first and foremost being able to show love to myself. But let's be clear here. Self-love isn't defined by having the occasional massage or pedicure. It's taking the time to be you, whatever that means. It's taking time to think, enjoy, laugh, and be still. I didn't even know what self-love was. Then I asked the question "What would I do for someone I love?" Aha!

LOVE IS A MOVING TARGET

Now, while I have never outright told a woman to leave her marriage, I have coached many women to find their own worth, find their own strength, and stand up for themselves. I have coached women on finding their God-given worth so that they can protect themselves and their children. I have coached myself into leaving my marriage, staying in my marriage, and leaving it again, all within the same conversation.

Even when professionals coached me into finding my own definition of love and how that played into my decision to stay or go, the answer was different at different times. Sometimes I wanted to stay, sometimes I wanted to leave, and sometimes I didn't know what I wanted. Most of the time, due to my devout Catholic upbringing, my answers were in line with my religious beliefs. However, there were many times when those beliefs were not congruent with my situation. There were times when I was certain that the women in the Bible could not possibly have dealt with the modern-day shitshow that I was living. In the Bible, women are taught to follow their husbands blindly; but my household felt so out of control sometimes that I was certain the teachings were developed by men who did not cheat or suffer from untreated mental illness (both of which I've dealt with in my marriage). More importantly, evolution has taught us that divorce is a process of the evolved. If you are fighting to eat, as a social tribe species, you are not thinking of divorce. Go to Third World countries, where marriage is a way to stay in the tribe and makes the difference between living and dying. Love may evolve, but the institution is entered into for survival.

Again, there is no award for the spouse who can live in misery the longest, but there are times when leaving the marriage, either for a short time or permanently, is the only option available to you.

I've become an expert at living with a spouse who challenges my resolve to stay married. There have been moments for me, and there may be moments for you, when you have to answer the question "should I go?" with "yes, I want out!" simply because it is the only way to save your own sanity. Yet maybe you don't mean that. It is okay. I am going to keep reminding you throughout this book that it is okay to hold onto your own reality as it happens. There are times when the only way you can save yourself, your children, and even your spouse is to set boundaries, stick to them, and leave.

A STORY OF MENTAL ILLNESS AND BROKEN VOWS

We delude ourselves into staying when we shouldn't stay because our brain and the software that it runs on is not designed to make us happy. As Dr. Daniel Amen writes in *Change Your Brain, Change Your Life*, "Don't believe all the stupid thoughts in your head."

Your brain is designed to keep you alive. It's done it for two million years and that remains its main function. Your mind copes with feelings that you should leave by literally looking the other way each time your spouse does something horrific. It has allowed you to protect yourself by lying to yourself. Just know, it's not the essence of who you are that does this—it's the software. I know because my brain's software allowed me to lie to myself for almost a decade by turning a blind eye to some abominable behaviors.

In the introduction to *Cry All You Want*, I talked about discovering my husband's battle with bipolar disorder in a very roundabout way. After we were married, it took us fifteen years to correctly diagnose and treat his disorder. Since I found out that he was bipolar when I was 22, I really had no context for what it meant to have a mental illness, especially one of that magnitude. What it meant was that his behaviors were erratic, sometimes abusive, unpredictable, and often very expensive.

Due to my naivete, I would often look the other way when Terry took an entire week off work to sleep or stayed up all night binge-watching TV only to call in sick the next day. I looked the other way because I had just finished college—where poor life choices were never ridiculed! I just thought we would all eventually grow up.

As I began to mature, I learned that Terry's poor life choices had real life consequences. I learned that the Prozac under his bathroom sink was not like Tylenol—to be taken when needed—but that it needed to be taken every day, without fail. As I grew up, I learned that the potential for danger in my relationship was real. Even though I knew in my bones that he would never physically hurt me, his actions were not in alignment with that gut feeling. My brain did to me what our brains do to all of us. It allowed me to believe what I kept telling myself: "It's not that bad."

MY BRAIN DID TO ME WHAT OUR BRAINS
DO TO ALL OF US. IT ALLOWED ME TO
BELIEVE WHAT I KEPT TELLING MYSELF:
"IT'S NOT THAT BAD."

As I continued to mature, I learned that when Terry pouted and left a party, it could mean that a dangerous situation was waiting for me at home. There were nights when I would come home to a loaded gun on the dresser and him passed out in the bed. As I got older and wiser, I learned that there was no level of fixing that I could personally do in that situation. I learned that I needed professional help to understand his illness and that he needed professional help to manage it.

While my husband was never physically abusive, living in my home was often a regular hell. Although I was never alone, I suffered from manifested loneliness. You know those times when you have someone sitting right next to you, but social media is more engaging? In fact, anything is more connected than the soul that's right in front of you. So there was the loneliness and then there was the disregard for our well-being. There were times when my husband would overspend to the point that it would take months for me to dig us out of the massive debt he'd accrued. There were times when my husband would let vital things like insurance lapse. Despite my comfortable career, there were years when we were on the cusp of ruin and it felt like the house of cards could fall at any moment. Still, my brain (that lovely software) would say, "It's not that bad. It could be worse." The social tribe species kept me in delusion. While society has evolved from the Stone Age to smartphones, the software that runs the human brain has not evolved.

Terry's disease led to more than just compulsive spending and the usual textbook issues that coincide with bipolar disorder (intense mood swings, manias and depressions, etc.). It also led to infidelity and to my husband having emotional affairs with other women. While I was studying for the bar exam, I knew that he was talking to other women. He would lock his phone around me and take it into the bathroom when he was showering. This was back in the days when mobile phones were just that—mobile telephones. Once, during my bar exam prep class, I found myself bored and violated my own privacy boundaries by checking his email. The term "checking" is used loosely . . . because I hacked it. What did I find? Dozens of nude photos from his "friend." What did I do? I packed up my stuff, took off to my uncle's remote cabin, took the exam, asked for a divorce (for the first time, other times to come), and drank way too much. My brother-in-law found me passed out on my living room floor after the binge. I assure you that I never did that again, because my joining the chaos was sure to ruin what I had started in my career. I now don't drink at all.

When I think back, that wasn't the first time that I noticed that behavior. One evening when I met him at his soccer league just after we were married, a woman came up to us and said, "I didn't know you were dating anyone." Little did she know—we had just gotten married two weeks earlier!

I did hit a breaking point eventually and told Terry that he needed to leave. It was either going to be in a police car or an ambulance—the choice was his. Fifteen years of tolerating his bipolar disease made his presence in the home intolerable for me. Our kids were getting older—we have twins together and he has an older daughter—and hiding his unstable behavior was getting harder and harder. I thought, "I'm not going to allow our son to grow up thinking that his father's behavior is okay. This is not how you treat your wife and kids."

Most of the time, my husband had two lives: The one that looked good on paper and in Christmas cards with me—the one that his parents would approve of—and the other one. This was the one that I chose not to see or share for many years. Our marriage was a roller coaster, and not the fun kind. I would demand change, he would promise to get help, and we would make up for a week or two. Things would seem better, but before long, the old patterns returned. Despite all of the promises, there was no real help, no real change, and no follow-through.

When I found myself joining Terry in his depression, I recognized that I could no longer keep the house of cards standing. I knew that if I let myself stay in the darkness with him, my business would crumble, our children would suffer, and there would not be a shovel strong enough to dig me out. I had to leave. I had to cry—and girl, did I cry—but then I knew it was time to get it done. I knew that my future needed light and hope. I couldn't stand by waiting for the swirl of the cyclone around me to whoosh me in. I had to go, I had to run, and I did.

I HAD TO CRY—AND GIRL, DID I CRY—BUT THEN I KNEW IT WAS TIME TO GET IT DONE.

At that point in time, there was just no more place in my life for my husband's anger. The space inside of me and inside of our home was overflowing, and something had to change. For me, change meant that I no longer wanted to carry the weight of everything all by myself. It meant that Terry would have to be consistent with his psych medicines and consistently go to his therapist. I wanted him to take the lead on managing his own mental health, and I didn't want to live with someone who was so miserable. I said to him, "I haven't slept in fifteen years. You need to change, because I need peace. This is not a buffet—you don't get to pick and choose which of these things you will change. You have to do them all, consistently, and forevermore."

I sold my home and all the contents within it. I rented a small house with enough space for me and my kidlets. I then bought my own house, in my name only to start protecting my assets (more on this later). I made it clear that I was done, and in my head and heart, I was. It was then that our old relationship died. In the agony of knowing that he would lose his kids—because no judge on Earth would allow him custody in his present state—he got help and followed through. It is crucial to note that he didn't get help for me, for us, or for the kids. He got it for himself. The lesson here for you is that if you need something to change, change it. If your spouse needs to change, he has to come to that conclusion and do the work on himself. There is nothing that you can do to help him if he does not want help. Making counseling appointments will not help if he does not want to be there.

Terry finally went for help. I don't know why that point in time finally made him do it, but it did. We quickly learned that his issues resulted from a brain injury that he had suffered, that presented like bipolar disorder. With this new information, he was more at ease. However, I clearly remember saying while driving up the California coast on the way back from the neurologist's office: "If you are asking me to allow you to be an asshole to me the rest of our lives because you have a brain injury, my answer is a 'hard pass.'"

I was willing to stand by him through his medical treatment during our separation, but I was not going to accept the life sentence if it meant that his unacceptable behavior would continue forever.

I don't know what changed after that last trip to the specialist, besides that Terry agreed to get the help that he needed, on his own accord, and to change the things that needed to change. He did the work that I knew was possible and I accepted his efforts. Now, have things been perfect? Not even close. Are things still challenging? For sure! Is his brain injury healed? Certainly not. But we are working together. We told each other what we needed out of the relationship. We chose to accept each other for who we are and to demand the best version of ourselves to show up every single day. Will Smith said it best, "I take care of myself for you, you take care of yourself for me." We also now have an agreement that if either wants to leave the relationship, we will earnestly not hate each other. We will earnestly work together to be fair and do what is best to raise our kids. We also have agreements surrounding our finances.

I need to add that my family's journey through this mental illness was difficult, but all the while Terry was suffering along with me. He didn't want or intend to act the way he was acting. I am not trying to demonize Terry or further stigmatize mental illness by telling my story. Instead, the genesis of my story was the genesis of this book and why as women we need to share what our lives are really like. Certainly, over the course of our marriage, I have also made mistakes, and when these situations happened, I ran away to my work. Throughout this, Terry was still very much a father, son, and friend. He is a good man. I tell my story as an example to show that you can overcome anything.

If you want to stay, if you decide that you have another round in you, then it's time to work on yourself. If you want something different, you need to do something different. So where do you start? Whether you stay or whether you go, your life is about to change. I often hear women say they just want things to go back to normal. But you can't go back. There is no back. That road is closed. You have to start from now, and from now on you must make different choices to produce different results.

IF YOU WANT SOMETHING DIFFERENT, YOU NEED TO DO SOMETHING DIFFERENT.

YOU'VE GOT NEEDS. HOW DO YOU MEET THEM?

Tony Robbins, who is one of my mentors, has created the following technology to understand human needs. We all have these six human needs[3]:

1. **Certainty:** assurance you can avoid pain and gain pleasure

2. **Uncertainty/Variety:** the need for the unknown, change, new stimuli

3. **Significance:** feeling unique, important, special, or needed

4. **Connection/Love:** a strong feeling of closeness or union with someone or something

5. **Growth:** an expansion of capacity, capability, or understanding

6. **Contribution:** a sense of service and focus on helping, giving to, and supporting others

One interesting thing about these needs is that we all fulfill them in different ways.

If you can relate at all, now is the time to look for mentors, teachers, and scholars for information and guidance on how to bring about lasting change in your life. This book is the beginning.

If you want to stay in your relationship, take the evaluation test in the resources section to determine how well you are meeting your human needs. Are you meeting your needs in a way that is productive or destructive? Take some time to understand your own brand of sabotage. Decide if you are leaving the relationship because it is time to leave or because you just don't know how to meet your needs another way. In each of my client's situations, they need to get leverage on themselves first to save their marriage, and both participants need to do the work.

3 Tony Robbins website – add citation

Now, even if you have already left the marriage in an epic fashion, if leaving isn't right for you, it can still be salvaged.

Drama Is Only Good for Television

At the start of one case, my client and her spouse inadvertently bought themselves several appearances on the nightly news with their ludicrously bad behavior. Both were public figures, so the news stations were happy to oblige. These two defined the word "DRAMA" in capital letters. If they had known a reality show producer, their drama would have quickly become a household hit. But despite the level of dysfunction, there was also a deep, mutual passion between them. They did not "hate" each other; they just each had careers where winning was all that mattered, and they were both employing the tools needed in their C-suites, but not in their marriage. And yes, mistakes had been made, along with some very poor life choices. What made it even worse was that both sides of their families were engaged in the drama, and in many instances fueled the fire even more. Then life happened for them.

During their divorce case, the judge required some procedural maneuvers that led to the case coming to a complete standstill. Both parties were furious because the tension of the situation was what was holding each together as a person. During that "cooling off" period, the drama died, because there were no courtroom tactics that could be slung in either direction and the media was not interested in a story where nothing was happening. During this cooling off period, which occurred when the COVID-19 pandemic was raging, their child became very ill and required extensive medical care. It was when they were sitting in the hospital waiting room, alone together, cut off from the news and their families' opinions, that they realized how insane their evening news appearances were. They both realized that they didn't want to end the relationship; they just wanted to end the drama. They also realized that what each needed most was compassion from the other and not judgment. That was when they figured out they could have the same high level of passion, but without the destruction. They decided they could meet their needs as a couple in a positive way.

After the cooling-off period, the case was dismissed because this couple decided that commitment to each other was more powerful than anything else. They also brought their families, who wanted nothing more than to see a win, into the reconciliation process. But the ultimate win was for their child, who needed each of them focused on his health and not the drama of the situation. It took telling everyone around them to just shut up so that they could hear themselves think and feel what they needed to feel. Now they are a silent, united force. Their little guy rallied, and his illness might have saved them all. They eventually divorced, but did so quietly, at peace, with fairness, with integrity, and as friends.

In a sense, the pandemic saved their divorce, because they needed solitary confinement in the hospital to find some space to think and feel. Now, even though they had decided to leave the marriage, after that experience, they did so without the manifest drama and theatrics.

If you decide that now is not the time, it is just fine to stay. It is okay to fight for a relationship that anyone outside of the relationship does not understand. In my situation, as I said, I wanted out. I wanted freedom. I needed peace. I needed rest—not the kind of rest that comes from sleeping late on a quiet Sunday morning, but the rest that comes from a peaceful home life. I simply had no more fight in me. It took leaving the relationship, buying my own house, and moving out for the light to finally shine where it needed to in order to show the cracks in the relationship. I decided exactly what I needed to stay in the relationship and my husband eventually stepped up to the challenge.

IT IS OKAY TO FIGHT FOR A RELATIONSHIP THAT ANYONE OUTSIDE OF THE RELATIONSHIP DOES NOT UNDERSTAND.

UNHEALTHY MEN

If you are with an unhealthy man, I still won't tell you to leave, but I will help you get some perspective and strength to make the best decision that you can. There are many types of unhealthy partners. There are cheaters, who are emotionally unhealthy. Then there are addicts, abusers, gaslighters, and those with a mental pathology that is dangerous.

A true definition of "unhealthy man" was developed by Alison Armstrong, a renowned expert on men, relationships, and communication with the opposite sex. According to Armstrong, an unhealthy man is one who physically or emotionally hurts his woman and children and does not protect them. It is that simple. Men are genetically wired[4] to protect their families. Unhealthy men do not have this genetic wiring.

Terry was unhealthy according to a medical, technical definition. However, he was not unhealthy in Armstrong's framework, because even through it all, he would have protected me and the children and never intended hurt. I understand what it's like to live within this dynamic and the guilt that is associated with wanting to disassociate with that man. But I'll tell you again, it's your relationship and it's your decision whether to stay or leave.

In every example I can think of, it took both parties taking massive action and starting from scratch to build a new future. This is not an effort that can happen with one person carrying the load. Both of you need to want it, both of you need to do anything and everything, so long as it is legal, to save the relationship. There may be doubt that it is possible, but I am sure you have surprised yourself in the past and can surprise yourself now.

If you are going to save the relationship, the lifeboat has two paddles and you both need to row in the same direction. It is not easy, but neither is divorce, so choose your hard. Remember, no one gets an award because they suffered the most. Choose what you want and then go after it.

4 https://greatergood.berkeley.edu/article/item/are_women_more_compassionate_than_men

"We either make ourselves
miserable, or we make
ourselves strong.
The amount of work
is the same."

—CARLOS CASTANEDA

CHAPTER 3

Separation Hurts—Divorce Doesn't Have To

Persistence is nothing more than the emotional journey toward creating something good. If you have made the decision that your marriage is coming to its end, then the only way to conquer the island is to burn your boats behind you. The hardest part is leaving. The second hardest part is the first night alone, the first weekend alone when you drop the kids off at your ex's house, the first holiday alone. The separation part can be brutal, but the process of divorce doesn't have to be. In most states, divorce is about math, business, and what is best for the children. The divorce court does not care about your pain. And those painful emotions can seriously detract from your ability to gather the evidence that you need.

PERSISTENCE IS NOTHING MORE THAN THE EMOTIONAL JOURNEY TOWARD CREATING SOMETHING GOOD.

As a wise judge once told me, "When you end a relationship, you will either be the carrot or the celery." As I stood there perplexed, she explained.

If it's truly the end, you can break cleanly apart like the carrot or you can break into shreds like the celery. One is clearly less painful than the other. Your life will never be the same again, so why not choose the clean break?

Now that you have made your decision to divorce, I am going to be brutally honest. You cannot move forward by relying on your current thought process. When people get divorced, they feel stress and anxiety and other levels of intense emotions. However, you cannot solve problems if you are not clear or are coming from an emotional place. If you are going to play with lions, you must become one. To get the most out of this process, you need to change your thinking. You need to think from a place where you're considering the outcome, not emotion.

PUT YOUR EMOTIONS ASIDE (AT LEAST WHILE YOU'RE IN THE COURTROOM)

The hardest news that I deliver to my newly divorcing clients is that they need to get ready for the battle of their lives. Imagine telling someone who is already feeling down and depleted that they still need to fight. It's hard to fight when you are already down on the ground. Not all divorces end up in battle; however, there are many nasty divorce lawyers who buy into the drama that a battle is inevitable. But in a good divorce, there is no winner and no loser, just an end. My hair stylist put this best: "We are bad bitches that fall and get back up."

Even if you know in your soul that your decision to leave is the best decision you could make, you'll still feel some level of pain and uncertainty during the divorce process. For many women who are very powerful in the boardroom, transferring this power to their personal life is hard, especially during divorce.

No matter who you are, as you embark on the divorce process, your emotions will not help to keep you financially secure. As you work through the next chapters, I ask you to table your feelings so that you can set yourself up for financial success. There will be plenty of time in this book to address how you can cope with your emotions to manage your outcome, but we are not going to start there. You have already done the work to make your decision to end the relationship. Now let's get your armor ready for battle.

> NO MATTER WHO YOU ARE, AS YOU
> EMBARK ON THE DIVORCE PROCESS,
> YOUR EMOTIONS WILL NOT HELP TO
> KEEP YOU FINANCIALLY SECURE.

As we go forward, I ask you to hold your finances in one hand (this includes what your financial life will look like the day after the judge signs the order). In your other hand, hold your emotions.

THE DATE EXERCISE

You may be wondering, "How can a lawyer tell me to separate my emotions from my finances when they are so intertwined?" In fact, they are not at all intertwined, although it is hard to see that when you're sitting in your lawyer's office and your life is changing rapidly. I use the date exercise with my clients who are having trouble separating the pain of divorce from the clarity needed to secure their finances. Pain is a story of betrayal, not a reality that will help you maintain your lifestyle.

> PAIN IS A STORY OF BETRAYAL, NOT
> A REALITY THAT WILL HELP YOU
> MAINTAIN YOUR LIFESTYLE.

The exercise is simple. Take out a piece of paper and a calendar. You can use the calendar on your phone or any calendar where you can see the next few weeks or months. Now, pick a date on the calendar. Your choice can be arbitrary, but try to make the date in the near future and before your next meeting with your lawyer, or the next deliverable that you have for your divorce case. If you haven't hired an attorney yet, pick a date before that process starts. Then put the date in the calendar in front of you and write down "FREE RENT ENDS."

This is the date when you will no longer give your spouse free rent in your mind. On this date, you will no longer allow your ex to control all of your thoughts. This is the day when you will liberate yourself from wondering what the other person will do, say, or think in any given situation. This is the day when you will take back your mind to make your own decisions. This is the day when you give yourself permission to divorce the story and marry your future. This is the day when you will understand that the finances sitting in one hand are the reality, and the emotions sitting in the other hand are the story.

The moment that you stop giving your ex free rent is the moment that you stop giving him any control over your valuable future. It is the moment when you say, "I will not allow my spouse to haunt my thoughts every waking minute of every living day." It is the moment when you set the worry aside and prepare yourself to get the outcome that you need—whether it be the house, retirement accounts, the business, or primary custody of your kids. It is the moment when you finally stop abusing your valuable time and find a lawyer that can guide you and get you the outcome that you desire.

Oftentimes, this exercise makes my clients skeptical. Most think that I am crazy. They ask—incredulously—"You're telling me that when I wake up on the date that I've chosen, the agony will be over?" My short answer is "yes." There is no one else on Earth who tells you what to think, what to feel, or when to decide something or not decide something but you. You inflict all of that punishment on yourself. Therefore, if you *decide* that you are no longer going to give the pain dominion in your life, then that's it. It's over. You have already decided that the marriage is over (or it has been decided for you), so now focus on the things that you can control instead of those that you cannot. You can control yourself—you cannot control what your partner does. Only you can control your emotions. Only you can decide to enter the divorce process with eyes wide open.

You need to replace those compulsive thoughts about your ex with something. This is the time to stand guard at the gates of your mind and start listening to the smartest people that you can find. Look for podcasts from proven leaders. I turned to Alison Armstrong, Tony Robbins, Joe Dispenza, and an epic app called NuCalm. I literally had to train my brain back into a place of peace. Like an infant, I needed to learn how to put myself to sleep again and allow myself to sleep. Ending the free rent is not enough; you need to replace the time and thoughts with something else.

DON'T LET FREE RENT DERAIL YOU

The saddest days in my entire career occur when the free rent exercise leads my clients into obsessive thoughts. *I must do this now.* I must do this tomorrow. Sometimes you're just not ready. Understand that you are human and may need to set more than one date. If you can differentiate your feelings about the separation from the written math problem called divorce, you will fare much better in this process. If you cannot, seek professional help. It's really okay.

The divorce process will have a beginning, a middle, and an end. Many of the clients I meet with are understandably depressed at the onset of the divorce process—some over the loss of the marriage, some over the loss of their children on weekends, some over the loss of financial security. Some let sadness become anger. Some let it manifest into complete compulsive psychosis. These are the emotions that can and should stay in one hand so the divorce process can move forward with the other hand. You will need to get a different kind of help for that. If your thoughts have created a medical condition, you need to seek medical advice to manage the health issue. However, many women can just make the conscious decision to start having some domain over their unconscious and automatic thoughts about the ex, what he will think, etc.

Client Story

The Good Dad Painted as Bad

Early in my career, before I had the skills that I have now, I witnessed a tragic loss that was the result of untreated depression. As a young lawyer, I knew one thing: Winning. My client was a good man who was in terrible pain. He had grown up in foster care and was terrified of losing his children. He loved his children dearly, but he did not have the tools to handle his depression alone. His case was particularly difficult as he had married a woman who was morally bankrupt. She first claimed that he would yell at the kids. When that didn't get the results that she wanted in court, she claimed that he would brutally spank the children. At that turn, we proved her absolutely wrong in court. Then she pushed the nuclear button and alleged that he had molested their daughter. She forced the child to go through so many forensic examinations that the physicians on the specialized Child Abuse Response Team refused to evaluate the child again unless it was ordered by the judge. Even worse, the judge found that the mother's actions were abusive, since none of the examinations showed any abuse. During all of this, my client was required to have supervised visits with his children. He went through countless evaluations himself to prove that he was a fit parent. While we were winning the court case, he was silently losing his battle with depression. He couldn't cope with the fact that, as a child abuse survivor himself, he was being accused of child abuse.

I vividly remember the call from his new partner. I always took her calls because she was the calm in his storm. This time, I could tell that she had been crying. I put on my coach hat to get to the bottom of the tears. She told me that she had been awakened in the middle of the night by a gunshot. She went to find out what was going on and found her husband's body in their backyard. He had left a note saying that he just couldn't fight any longer.

This was someone who was struggling with depression and needed help. This was a tragedy that could have been avoided. I want you to hear and believe these words: THIS CASE IS NOT WORTH YOUR LIFE. No matter the demons in your head right now, there is a compelling future for you. If the loss of this marriage, of public stature, of income—or the embarrassment of court—has you thinking that you cannot fight anymore, then you are not fighting a divorce battle, you are fighting a depression battle. Take these thoughts seriously and get help immediately.

There is no "fight to the death" in divorce. There are ways to get what you want and need, and to get what is fair. In no divorce court in America are you judged for seeking help when you need it. It's okay to talk to a therapist. It's okay to go on antidepressants. It is even okay to take drastic steps like removing firearms from your home. It's okay to get help. In no universe does honesty with a mental health professional work against you. I have seen over and over that the party who refuses help is treated more harshly than the party who recognizes the need for help and leans in fully to get it.

IT'S OKAY TO TALK TO A THERAPIST.
IT'S OKAY TO GO ON ANTIDEPRESSANTS.
IT'S OKAY TO GET HELP.

You have a right to a future; don't let anything get in the way of that. Get help now if you think this is the end of the road for you. We all have a highway to pain and a dirt road to happiness. Start to build that dirt road into a highway. And while you're at it, start building a new you—and before you know it, you'll have a new life. I have seen more than one case end in death and if I can help even one person find the distinction between divorce pain and depression pain, this entire book will have been worth it.

THE NEW YOU

The strongest force in human nature is to stay consistent with your identity. Whether you have defined your identity as a wife, mother, businesswoman, coach, gardener, cook, the hostess with the mostest—we strongly associate with our identities. However, be assured that when you get divorced, your identity will shift. Social media magnifies and reinforces the identity that you have created for yourself. You can post all those beautiful beach pictures of your family vacation to Hawaii because the camera can only face in one direction. Your friends on social media cannot see that the trip was miserable; that your spouse took his phone into the bathroom so he could text his mistress; that he was harsh with every word and dreadful to be around. Social media is what you want your reality to be, not what it is. So don't let the loss of those posts prevent you from re-creating your identity. In fact, delete your social media account. Call your closest friends and tell them that you are going through a divorce and if they want to invite you to something or share pics, they should message you.

SOCIAL MEDIA IS WHAT YOU WANT YOUR REALITY TO BE, NOT WHAT IT IS.

The sooner you recognize that you need a new identity, the easier the transition into single life will be. The tragic occurrence of suicidal clients is not novel. It happens more often than any divorce lawyer will admit. The root of the trauma is that the client is losing their identity—the labels they have allowed to define their life. The labels you have applied to yourself create your identity. As part of the divorce, you may be moving homes, moving businesses, selling properties, or selling businesses. Your children may be changing schools. You will probably have temporary court orders halting those glamorous events that lead to nice social media posts. These things will happen. The meaning that you assign to these events in your mind will matter. See them for what they are: Part of a process, not the end.

Client Story

The Socialite

One of my clients was part of the country club set. When she was going through her divorce, she held tight to her old identity as a country club regular. In fact, she was so adamant about keeping that identity that she lost her home.

Instead of downsizing and moving out of the neighborhood that served the country club, she held onto a $2 million home despite having only $30,000 in her bank account. The house was not paid off and she could not pay the mortgage.

At one point, she was 10 months behind on her mortgage and told me, "If I don't make $1 million in the next six months, I'll lose everything." What she wasn't willing to do was admit that she couldn't afford the house, the lifestyle, or her old identity.

So, how do you get around this type of situation? You created yourself once; you can create yourself again. Imagine if you woke up each morning and had the belief that you could create your future. What decisions would you make? How would you act? What would you do?

It is time for a massive reinvention. Let your old identity go. Then create something new, fresh, and vibrant that is whatever you want to be. My new identity included authoring this book.

Client Story

The Phoenix

One of my male clients had an incredible ranch in Colorado. When he and his wife divorced, she asked for the ranch. I didn't know how he would react to that since he had spent 50 years building the ranch and the business around it.

His wife told him that she wanted the ranch so that she could "retire," and he agreed. I couldn't believe it. He said, "I did it once before, I can do it again," meaning that he could build a business similar in scope on his own, again at an older age.

So, what did he do? He spent five years building a comparable ranch in Texas. Five years. That's all it took for him to build what he had spent 50 years building the first time around. His prior success left clues.

The meaning that you assign to your divorce is the meaning that it will have. It is okay to cry, but you still have to get it done. You are the biggest obstacle in the way of your own happiness. If you want to have an amazing life, then enjoy what is right in front of you.

IT'S A CHOICE, AND THE CHOICE IS YOURS

The claim that divorce doesn't have to hurt may sound unrealistic. But if you have the tools to handle your emotions, the actual process of divorce is not painful. Yet the shifting emotions during the process are real. The anger is apparent, the hurt is palpable, and uncertainty is driving the train. It seems so arbitrary to say, "Don't give free rent." It seems so arbitrary to pick a date to end the pain. It sounds like stupid advice. But according to my mentor, Tony Robbins, it's the same amount of work to make yourself miserable as it is to make yourself strong, so why not make yourself strong? The minute you realize that you control your thoughts and decisions in this situation—the minute you define this as the beginning or the end—you will take your power back.

No matter which state you live in, the process of divorce doesn't care about your emotions. The divorce judge does not care if you are heartbroken or if you did the heart breaking. In fact, to stay impartial, the judges cannot care. They cannot engage in the emotion of the divorce or even allow it to be present. If they did, we would need mental health sabbatical leave for judges.

NO MATTER WHICH STATE YOU LIVE IN, THE PROCESS OF DIVORCE DOESN'T CARE ABOUT YOUR EMOTIONS.

If you want the judge to hear about your awful ex who cheated on you, save it. The judge doesn't care. Your job is to stay completely focused on your outcome. Destroying the other person will not help you get your outcome, especially if what you say affects your ex's job. Saying something that can put them in jeopardy at work might mean they lose their job, and then what happens to your child support? You pay more!

Now, how do you stay focused on the process? It is a *business* process. Put your focus and energy on making a decision. If you are dealing with a physically or emotionally unhealthy divorce, due to mental illness, substance abuse, or domestic violence, there is an entire section on that later in the book.

Ms. Laser-Focused

I had one client who had millions at stake in her divorce. She came to me and said, "These are my hard stops. These are the things that I most want and will not budge on."

She was completely emotionless and told me to get it done and call her if I needed anything. It was such a big case that she ended up giving us power of attorney so that we could get the records that we needed and she didn't have to be involved.

In doing that, she removed herself from the process entirely. In the last 10 minutes of the trial, she left and said, "I'm walking out." She didn't walk out because she was a coward. She walked out because, for the first time during the case, she let herself cave to emotions. She was steadfast from beginning to end in terms of her outcome, but once she got that, she let her emotional self out.

This client got everything that she wanted and went on to create a really incredible identity for herself. She removed herself from the emotional pieces of the divorce and focused on outcome. She dealt with the emotions in one hand and the finances in the other.

YOU DESERVE BETTER

When I decided that I was going to leave my husband, I was headed out of town to a seminar about masculine and feminine energy. It was interesting. There were numerous discussions about how men need sex, freedom, and respect in a relationship while women need security, the ability to be seen and heard, and safety.

The featured topic on the last day of the seminar was "Relationship Day." It culminated in several couples getting engaged, oddly enough. Other couples who had been struggling found themselves reconciling. At the time, I felt that I had anything but a relationship. I was there (by myself) to learn how to exit a painful marriage, not save it. In short, I left the event feeling exhausted. I wanted nothing more than to get back to my hotel and sleep until my flight home.

Yet after it ended, I found myself waiting with a hundred other people in the cold for my Lyft. During the next 30 minutes, everyone had been picked up except for me and another woman. There were no cabs. Public transportation wasn't running at that hour. So, there I was, in the dark with a stranger in a wheelchair. We started talking as we waited. When my car eventually showed up, I offered her a ride to her hotel.

We loaded her wheelchair into the car and left. Her hotel was across town, but I didn't mind as we struck up an intriguing conversation. Our driver, who clearly had no social skills, asked her bluntly if she'd always been paralyzed. Sitting mortified in the back seat, but equally nosy, I listened in. She'd been in a terrible accident that had taken her ability to walk. After her accident, her relationship had broken up. At first, she was angry at God and her friends. Her life contracted into one word: Anger. As we drove through Palm Beach alongside the ocean, I listened to every word. I had just spent $10,000 on a seminar to learn how to be happy, and her anger was exactly what I felt. I asked her what brought her to the seminar, because this was generally not a place for angry people. She explained that she was not angry anymore. I asked, "How? What changed? How did you go from suffering a terrible sense of loss to being this happy person?" She answered, "I decided not to be angry anymore. I made the decision to be grateful each day." She simply decided not to let the negative emotions of her life control her future. She simply decided to have something different.

Of course, that decision did not mean that she'd regain the use of her legs, but it did mean that she was not going to let that lack hold her back or control her emotions. She was going to live life to the fullest with no regard for her physical limitations. She was very confident and very matter-of-fact. I realized that I had let the anger over my marriage contaminate every other area of my life. I realized that if she could decide to have something different, so could I.

I REALIZED THAT IF SHE COULD DECIDE TO HAVE SOMETHING DIFFERENT, SO COULD I.

After we dropped her off at her hotel, I rode silently in the back of the Lyft, pondering the idea that a decision was all that was in the way of my own happiness. It was there that I decided what my life would be going forward. I told myself that I could decide to accept my husband as he is with just one thing: A decision. All night, I pondered the woman's courage to decide. I journaled about all the decisions I had made in the past that had led me to my epic pity party, and all the decisions I could make in the future that would instantly end the suffering of expectations of a love that didn't pan out.

Did it change my financial picture, my health, or my problems? Did it instantly make my husband a kinder human? Not at all. However, it was a tool that I used to approach a lion in my life. Who thought your life could change in a Lyft? Like her, you too can make a decision to be happy, to end your suffering, and to feel gratitude instead of pain. You can decide if this divorce is the beginning or the end.

Now every day I do the following:

- I make a conscious effort to say what I'm grateful before I leave the house in the morning. You cannot be angry and grateful at the same time. Try it—it doesn't work.
- Gratitude is at the forefront of my mind when I go to bed at night and when I wake up in the morning.

I keep sticky notes on my desk that encourage me to "decide the outcome, develop it, deliver it, and celebrate it."

I remind myself that I can't be grateful and suffer at the same time.

YOU DECIDE HOW TO FEEL

If you believe that you have nothing to be grateful for, walk through this next exercise with me. First read this, then close your eyes, take a deep breath, and put your hand on your heart. Do you feel a heartbeat? If the answer is yes, then you have plenty to be grateful for. If you want to feel this same gratitude for parenting your child, even through divorce, do the same exercise, but this time, place your hand on your child's heart and realize that as long as there is a heartbeat, you can handle this process that you are going through. I do this exercise every morning. If I am conscious of the fact that I have a heartbeat and that I am on the right side of the grass, then today I will find gratitude, no matter what the courtroom throws at me. On days that I am not feeling it, I use the NuCalm app and force the gratitude to appear.

IF I AM CONSCIOUS OF THE FACT THAT I HAVE A HEARTBEAT AND THAT I AM ON THE RIGHT SIDE OF THE GRASS, THEN TODAY I WILL FIND GRATITUDE, NO MATTER WHAT THE COURTROOM THROWS AT ME.

You ask, "How is it possible to simply decide not to have pain when it feels like the pain is keeping you alive?" I answer, "Because your brain is not designed to make you happy. It is designed to keep you alive. So the sooner you get control of it, the easier this process will be." Your mind also takes everything personally, which means that perception is projection. That means that if you think your ex is an asshole, you might be the one behaving like an asshole. What you perceive is what you project. So, project something different. If you want your divorce to be better, then you need to be better. If you want a better co-parent, then do your best to be a better co-parent. If you want an apology from your spouse, maybe you owe the apology. You own your mind; it does not own you. Somedays, I scream this at myself—"I own you!"—because then I make my mind stop the destructive chatter.

How can you make this decision and assign the meaning that you desire to the divorce process? If you tell yourself that the process sucks, then it will suck. If you tell yourself that this is the worst thing that's ever happened to you, then it will be. If you tell yourself that your children will be ruined, then that might be the case. The story that you tell around your divorce matters. The words that you use to describe this process also matter. If you tell yourself that this is a business transaction that you need to finalize with as little pain and as few attorney's fees as possible, then that can be your reality.

Remember, the words you declare become the house that you live in.

THE STORY THAT YOU TELL AROUND YOUR DIVORCE MATTERS. THE WORDS YOU DECLARE BECOME THE HOUSE THAT YOU LIVE IN.

Therefore, decide to be happy, decide what your future will look like, decide if this is the beginning or the end. Decide if this divorce is going to be the most painful thing that you have ever endured, or a necessary step to find what is true and meaningful in your life. Decide if you are going to curl up into a ball every time you need to talk to your lawyer, every time your ex's number crosses your notification bar, or if you are going to approach this process with power. Decide if co-parenting is going to ruin your children or make them resilient and dynamic. Decide if you will stay on the high road where you can see the cliffs and the danger, or in the ravine where you are the victim of whatever comes for you. The high road is always a more beautiful drive. Yes, this process can be tolerable as you follow the path to your new life. The first morning alone might feel lonely, but it might also feel liberating and peaceful. Only you can make that decision. Now that you have your mindset in order, turn the page and let's talk money.

"I love cash and cash loves me."

–KEITH CUNNINGHAM

CHAPTER 4

The Honest Financial Audit (The Joneses Are Not Watching)

L et's start with the truth: You cannot have in divorce what you do not already have. Everything that is financed in the house of cards ends now. If you have debt, or your standard of living or lifestyle does not exist except for on credit, the court cannot protect it. If you have debt, the Louis Vuitton on your arm and Christian Louboutins on your feet are not owned by you; they are owned by your American Express. You need to look at the real numbers and decide for yourself if your house is made of sticks or made of bricks. In the prior chapters, we talked about the absolute importance of getting real with your emotions. Now it's time to get real with the numbers.

Client Story
Lashes

It's hard to present reality to someone who cannot see their own. Once I had a client come in who was extremely upset about getting $4,000 a month in spousal support. We sat down and talked through her finances—what about that settlement wasn't working?

She had only an $1,800-a-month mortgage, yet while we sat there, she told me she was going to have to move out and let the house go into foreclosure because she couldn't afford to keep it. Doing the math, this didn't make a whole lot of sense to me. But then I noticed that she had a $4,500 purse. And, as we dug deeper, I learned that she got her nails done every other week—same with her lashes. She told me these things while tapping one of her Donald Pliner shoes against my desk. I know how much those shoes cost because I've been wanting to buy a pair myself—not cheap and I couldn't afford them.

Then she asked me to discount her legal fees and I said, "You're losing your house over poor financial decisions." It was tough to bring her to the realization that she was making choices, those choices have results, and her results were negative.

If you break down the financial process in divorce, it is all about what you own and what you owe, and if you don't own something—if your life has been built on credit—you won't have anything.

Now, if you are not a numbers person or have deferred to your husband to "handle things," repeat after me: "I love cash and cash loves me." You must learn this. You must understand cash or the wolf will come and blow your house away. You'd be surprised at the number of women—successful, smart women—who have no idea what their true financial situation is.

I had a client that was devasted when I told her that her alimony award could not possibly be what she wanted to live on. She insisted that it simply could not be right. She had an expert that told her how much money she needed to live comfortably. Over and over, I was berated over the fact that she lived on triple that amount in the marriage and I simply was not doing my job because I didn't get her more money. In this case, she had filed for bankruptcy prior to the divorce. She signed the bankruptcy, but seemed unaware of its effects. They were not living on earnings; they were living on the reputation of good credit. As I started to dig, I learned that she had discharged over a half million dollars in credit card debt. How could either of them get spousal support? It is impossible for a judge to give you what you don't already have. None of it was real now and it never was real to begin with. It was the illusion of credit.

As Americans, we are SAD, with the "standard American desire." We want bigger and better cars; we want to live in a nice neighborhood and send our children to nice schools. We Americans were born in the greatest nation on Earth and expect to be rewarded for that birthright.

THE PUBLIC HOUSE OF CARDS

As women, and women who have "made it," we have grown accustomed to nice things. A new designer bag and Mercedes Benz are standard fare for our diet. We like and deserve nice things. In many circles, the stuff is the status. The stuff is the significance. Having to lose the stuff or make an honest disclosure about the debt incurred to have said stuff is a second punch in the gut.

If this resonates with you, it might be time to admit that you have not saved as much as you wanted, or worse, that the bankruptcy powder keg is about to blow. What makes this even more gut-wrenching is that in some states, financial disclosures are public records, so everyone can see what you pay and who you pay. I've definitely had clients who have been embarrassed by their spending and the fact that they were public record.

When you go through a divorce, not only will your house of cards become apparent, but it also might be very public.

> IF YOU BREAK DOWN THE FINANCIAL
> PROCESS IN DIVORCE, IT IS ALL ABOUT
> WHAT YOU OWN AND WHAT YOU OWE.

If you don't love cash or are not interested in keeping more of it, then you can skip this chapter. If you in fact, like me, love cash, then let's take a deep dive to see where the money is. Money is not the root of all evil and it's not just money. You can cry all the way home from divorce court on a bicycle or in your Mercedes. I don't have a big ego, but I do love fancy cars, and if my husband ever decides to leave me, he would need to run me over with my BMW to keep it.

This chapter is about honesty, and honesty is the hardest part of divorce. You need to be honest with yourself about why this is the best decision for you. More importantly, you need to face the mirror with the financial decisions that you have made to this point, and that's not always easy. You know what I am talking about. You know that there are times when you may have hidden the fact that the Prada bag in your closet was not a delicious gift from your best friend and your parents did not pay for that lavish weekend in Napa last year. You must face the fact that your credit report is going to be shared with your spouse and your lawyer. You knew that there was no harm in checking your credit limits toward the end of the month to get that last manicure, because after all, you would open some credit with a payment after payday. You and only you know what the real financial picture looks like.

IT'S ALL ABOUT THE MATH

Divorce is about math, so you can't be afraid of it. Take a deep gulp and swallow whatever bad financial decisions that you have made until now. Because after all, it's a new day, and you can't build a new future on the crumbled foundation of the past. That means: Do the audit, know where you stand, and know what you need.

> ### DIVORCE IS ABOUT MATH, SO YOU CAN'T BE AFRAID OF IT.

Now, the converse might be true: you might be swimming in cash. Most of my readers have likely been wildly successful—this is a book for achievers, after all. So even if your financial house is in order and built on bricks, you need to take the time to do the audit. Depending on your state or prenuptial agreements, you need to have a clear map to know where to place the X.

This is a scary part of any divorce. You consider, "What will my friends think if they knew the Prada bag was financed? What will my parents think when they find out that we have no retirement savings?" Here is the truth—nobody cares about any of that but you. You need to look in the mirror while you do the following exercise of diving into your finances, and do it in the solitude of your own home.

It is so easy to try to base our financial decisions on what our girlfriend got in her divorce. She got to keep the house; her alimony payment will set her up for the next 10 years so long as she doesn't get remarried. Or, she only had to pay two years of support of $500 per month whereas you are staring down the barrel of a $10,000-per-month payment. In divorce, you can't have what you don't have, and you can't give what you don't have. The only way to know what you have and what you can give is to take the deep financial dive.

IN DIVORCE, YOU CAN'T HAVE WHAT YOU DON'T HAVE, AND YOU CAN'T GIVE WHAT YOU DON'T HAVE.

You need to get this clear: If you don't know where you are, you don't know where you are going. If you don't know what you have, you don't know what you need. You cannot make good financial decisions without good financial information. A pilot cannot fly a plane without a dashboard—hell, you can't drive a car without a dashboard of numbers and dials that give you information to tell you which move to make next. Finances in divorce are no different. You need a dashboard.

It is time to go to confession with your lawyer and lay out the good, the bad, and the fact that you might have a massive stash of cash in Venmo and crypto. Your lawyer cannot protect you if they don't have a clear map of the territory. More importantly, you can't find the treasure if your map is covered with uncertainty.

In the divorce process, the lawyer is going to ask for tax returns, bank statements, paycheck stubs, etc. However, let's face it, the tax return is what the government knows about your financial status, and what your CPA found important to share with the government based on the Internal Revenue Service (IRS) rules. A tax return is not a good map of the territory.

Most courts have set rules on what you need to disclose and when. However, those rules are designed to educate the judge about your financial picture. They're not to educate you.

So, how do you start to create the right map? Start here. Here is your dashboard.

WHAT DO YOU OWN?

This is the first step in the exercise. Many of my clients cannot tell me what they own. They have lost track or do not remember. Especially in long-term marriages, it is hard to remember the valuables that are hidden within your estate.

Here is a broad list of places to start looking:

✓ Tax returns

✓ Household items

✓ Collectibles

✓ Automobiles

✓ Insurance documents

✓ Trust agreements—The attached schedules

✓ Real property records

✓ Physical toys, RVs, etc.

✓ Retirement accounts

✓ Insurance accounts

✓ Paid time off

✓ Health savings accounts

✓ 529 accounts

- ✓ Online investment accounts
- ✓ Businesses
- ✓ Notes payable
- ✓ Cryptocurrency accounts
- ✓ Loan applications
- ✓ App-based accounts
- ✓ Bank accounts

TAX RETURNS

Tax returns are an extremely useful tool to define what you own, but they are not gospel. They are an accumulation of things that your CPA found necessary to share with the IRS based on the tax code.

In your tax returns, you can find depreciation schedules for a business, which will provide a quick snapshot of valuable items that are currently owned. You need to look at current schedules and old schedules so that you can get a historical list of what you own. For example, if you own business equipment, after a certain number of years, that equipment will no longer appear on the tax returns because it no longer has value to the IRS. However, it will continue to be utilized in the business and may be sitting in the business lot with substantial value. It is helpful to look at these lists to start with those refences. Tax returns are a fairly accurate reflection of your and your spouse's income, which we will dive deeper into later in this chapter.

HOUSEHOLD ITEMS

It is really easy to forget that some of the art and jewelry in your home may have tremendous value. The Rolex watches that your spouse collected are considered household items. Your designer purse collection and shoes can also be considered assets. The easiest way to get a list of personal household items is to walk through the house and take a video of what is in each room. Then you can also start a handwritten list of various items. There are things of value that you want to make sure that you can keep, because replacing them is expensive. For example, my knife set cost more than my stove and refrigerator. If you are no longer in the house, look at old bank statements and try to recall what's in your home.

COLLECTIBLES

You'll want to make lists of sports memorabilia, wine collections, art collections, antiques, and other items that have resale value. I have worked on cases where the parties' collectibles were more valuable than their home. If you are not in the house, then get records from the sellers of the items.

AUTOMOBILES

This is simple. Get a snapshot of the registration for every vehicle that you are aware of and own. If you can find the title, great, but that is not generally necessary. If you can take a snapshot of the mileage on each vehicle, that will help with the valuations later. If you are not in the house, then contact your state's motor vehicle department, because they keep a list.

INSURANCE DOCUMENTS

If you are insuring it, you own it. You will want this for both your business and personal records. Also, if you are insuring something for $1 million, it will be tough to argue in court that it is worth less; therefore, look at limits of insurance and special riders. Know that your insurance documents are available from the brokers if you don't have access to the books.

TRUST AGREEMENTS

In most trust documents there is a schedule that shows all items that were funded into the trust. This document will help you remember where your assets are and help you find deeds to real property.

REAL PROPERTY

This is land and your house. This is anything that you own that is set on dirt. You'll want to make a list of addresses of all real property that you own. This can be your primary residence, vacation homes, or rentals.

Before you spring for an appraisal, ask a trusted real estate agent to prepare a market analysis—meaning, if they sold the house for you, what would they expect to list it for and what are comparable houses in your area selling for? If you don't have a list of properties, you can find them through city and county records.

> ## BEFORE YOU SPRING FOR AN APPRAISAL, ASK A TRUSTED REAL ESTATE AGENT TO PREPARE A MARKET ANALYSIS.

TOYS

This is where things get sticky. Usually in a marriage, one person loves and wants to keep the toys, which have value. This is the recreational vehicle, Jet Skis, airline miles, jet cards, and all the extras.

RETIREMENT ACCOUNTS

In looking for these, remember that there are 401(k) accounts and traditional IRAs, and then there are pensions. If you or your spouse works for the federal or state government, then you'll have both. The federal government has the Federal Employees Retirement System (FERS) and Thrift Savings Plan (TSP), so look for both. State governments usually have a pension and deferred compensation plan. The retirement accounts have a present value of moneys that you have saved, while the pensions do not have a present value that is readily available. Just because you cannot pinpoint the value does not mean that it does not exist. You want to work with a financial planner to understand your accounts and their present and future values.

INSURANCE ACCOUNTS

Life insurance will need to be valued in the divorce, and in many instances it is used to secure child support or spousal support payments.

You'll want to get a good clear list of available life insurance. In this exercise, do not forget to list group plans that either spouse has access to through employment. Look also for cash value in plans.

PAID TIME OFF

In many states, a spouse's accumulated paid time off is an asset to be divided in divorce. It's painful, but get a listing of paid time off (PTO) for division later. If you are the spouse with all the paid time off, use some of it to get this audit done and to get the rest you need for the battle ahead. Now is not the time to hoard PTO.

HEALTH SAVINGS ACCOUNTS

This is a place where people forget to look for assets. For example, I have clients with large numbers in these accounts, and since they don't look at it as something that they can spend, they forget that it's there.

529 ACCOUNTS

Your children's college savings accounts can be divided, but you'll want to list a future custodian of the account if it is currently a joint account. Therefore, get a listing of these accounts.

ONLINE INVESTMENT ACCOUNTS

Scottrade, E-Trade, Robinhood, and most brokerages have online portals for individual investing and trading. You want both the current balances and the historical balances to see if money has been moved.

BUSINESSES

Valuing businesses in divorce is a book of its own, but get a listing of all businesses started or sold during the marriage. Get tax returns and bank statements for each business. Meet with your CPA to get good information on the business assets and liabilities schedules. You will want historic and current profit and loss statements, balance sheets, and cash flow statements. People forget to ask for the cash flow statements, which is the real measure of a company's liquidity.

PERSONAL NOTES

The money that you lent to your sister last year may be considered an asset in the divorce to be divided, so make a list of all money that you are owed.

CRYPTOCURRENCY

You want to look for Coinbase, Gemini, and other accounts and apps that are used for buying and trading cryptocurrency. This will be much harder to track based on the current technology, but you can start with the major providers to look for accounts.

LOAN APPLICATIONS

This a great place to look for items of value that you have listed. For large loans, most banks require a personal financial statement, which includes a listing of assets and the values that you have assigned to those assets. You'll want to look at all loan applications for yourself and those that your spouse has filed.

APP-BASED ACCOUNTS

At one point, I had more money in my Venmo account than in my checking account. I simply forgot to transfer the Venmo money for a significant amount of time. You'll want to look into the values of Venmo, Cash App, PayPal, and Remitly accounts. There can be significant value sitting in those accounts.

BANK ACCOUNTS

It goes without saying that bank accounts will have keys to many puzzles if you have to protect your assets or save other assets. Be sure to look at credit union accounts and in other banks where you know there have been traditional accounts. There is software available to analyze spending, which may lead to assets.

This list is not exhaustive, but it will give you a start to get together a listing of items that you own. There is a worksheet provided in this book to help you fill in this simple OWN list.

WHAT DO YOU OWE?

This is not what do you spend, but what do you owe. We will get to spending a little later in this chapter. Figuring out what you owe is much easier than figuring out what you own. To do this, you'll need to look at:

- Credit reports
- Bank statements

CREDIT REPORTS

When I was in undergrad, I was so poor that I scrounged around in my car for a dime to buy a scantron to take my exams. I would literally buy one at a time. Couple that with the slew of credit card companies there to graciously greet me at college with their colorful and enchanting booths giving away free logoed koozies—you get the picture. I had the credit curse until sometime after law school. There came a point when I just stopped applying for credit because I didn't know what was in that dreaded report, but whatever it was and however you read it, it wasn't good. I know that it can be uncomfortable, but let's swallow hard and move forward.

Your credit report is the first place to start digging for what you owe. You would be shocked by how many clients are stunned to their core when they learn that their spouse went on a shopping spree using their credit . . . more than once. There are great services that will allow you to pull a three-bureau report. That means that all the bureau reports are side by side. Not all creditors report to all three credit bureaus so you cannot make an honest assessment with only one-third of the pie. Side note: The services will want to sign you up for credit monitoring. If there ever was a time in your life when it's not a bad idea to have some credit monitoring, during your divorce is that time. If you or your spouse misses a court-ordered credit payment, mortgage payment, etc., you will be alerted when it hits your report.

YOUR CREDIT REPORT IS THE FIRST PLACE TO START DIGGING FOR WHAT YOU OWE.

You need to do the same exercise with your spouse's credit report. In many cases, his debt is going to be your debt if it was incurred during the marriage.

I tell my young associates to check their partner's credit before they get married. Most look at me, astonished that I would suggest such an atrocity, but it's better before the church aisle than after in the court aisle.

In these reports, you're looking at your credit balances on each account. When going through these reports, ask yourself these questions:

1. How much do you owe? Hint: Enter it into an Excel spreadsheet or you can use the worksheets in the resource section at the end of this book. You can also go to my website (cryallyouwant.com) to download the worksheets.

2. What is the credit line on each account?

3. What are your interest rates on each account? In negotiations, you may be attached to the airline miles card, because it has the adorable picture of your pup, but it may be your highest-interest debt. When it comes to sharing that debt, the interest rate matters in your long-term financial plan, and not all debt is created equal.

4. Are you maxed out?

5. Are you familiar with all the accounts on the report? If not, thumb to the back of the report, get the creditor's contact information, and find out who opened the account, when, and if your signature was electronic.

In most states, you are going to need to complete comprehensive financial disclosures that include the addresses of your creditors. Your lawyer may need to subpoena financial statements from your spouse. This gem of the credit report will have all of your creditors' addresses, account numbers, and dates that the accounts were opened. The dates that the accounts were opened are so important if dividing debt in your divorce.

Now, if you are in the place where you have no debt, fantastic, but you need this information regardless. At some point, you likely did have debt. At some point, you bought a house, paid it off, etc. If you need to prove claims in your divorce, do this exercise. Also, don't make assumptions of what is in the report. I have seen too many people shocked in the end.

The credit report is the first place to get a quick financial glimpse. It is where you are going to start to determine whether your divorce strategy is going to be to off-load debt or secure cash assets, and how to divide what is owed and what is owned.

> # THE CREDIT REPORT IS WHERE YOU ARE GOING TO START TO DETERMINE WHETHER YOUR DIVORCE STRATEGY IS GOING TO BE TO OFF-LOAD DEBT OR SECURE CASH ASSETS, AND HOW TO DIVIDE WHAT IS OWED AND WHAT IS OWNED.

Unless your parents purchased your home for you and your spouse has no claims to it, or you otherwise have a sole and separate agreement, after the divorce, you are going to need a place to live. It might be the same place that you woke up this morning, but you will need to rearrange ownership and rearrange the debt to keep it. In addition to your lawyer, seek out the advice of a mortgage professional to review the report with you. Most banks and credit unions have a credit specialist on staff that is not there to sell you a loan but rather to educate you on your credit. Knowing what the score means for purchasing your current home, or new home, or even just being competitive in securing an apartment in a desirable neighborhood—this information is needed.

Do the same exercise with your spouse's credit report if you have legal access to it. If not, you can ask your lawyer to obtain it during the discovery process. But keep this on the list of items that you want to inspect yourself. Don't rely on anyone else to do the work for you.

If you own a business or your spouse owns a business, there is a credit report for the business. There are also financial statements for the business. Go through this exercise with the business accounts.

BANK STATEMENTS

Look through these to see what you are paying monthly toward debt. You can't get to your destination if you do not know where you are.

WHAT DO YOU SPEND?

It is really easy to remember that you live in a house and pay a mortgage on that house monthly. It is much harder and more sobering to analyze what you spend on a monthly basis. If you skip this exercise, you will have no idea what you actually need financially following the divorce, especially if you are a business owner or are self-employed. Many expenses are legitimate business expenses that need to be considered, but it is sobering how expensive lashes and nails are each month. It is even more astounding how fast Hulu and Netflix charges add up. If you need money right now—cut the extras. Cut hard and fast.

> IF YOU NEED MONEY RIGHT NOW—CUT THE
> EXTRAS. CUT HARD AND FAST.

For this exercise, get at least three months' worth of bank statements and look at where your money goes. Make a list of the recurring expenses withdrawn from your bank or charged to your credit card each month, and then make a list of other expenses. There is software that will do this for you. Many credit cards will give you the monthly pie chart snapshot that shows where your money generally goes—travel, restaurants, etc. While this is helpful, most people don't just spend on one card consistently. Therefore, you need to do this across the board. You'll want to gather all expenses, including utilities, school tuition, medical care, prescription costs, donations to your church—everything that you spend on a routine basis.

In the spend analysis, be sure to add up what is spent on your behalf by a business that you may be exiting as part of this divorce. If the business is paying your lease, insurance, cell phone, health insurance, and the like, then you need to add those expenses to your post-divorce budget. At the end of this book, there is a list of monthly expense items so that you can plan your budget.

Next add annual special events to your budget. This would be costs for the kidlets' birthday parties, Christmas gifts, and travel. These are annual expenses that are not routine.

In completing an honest financial audit, you should be able to have a clear picture of what you owe, what you own, and what you spend. When you have those things pinned, then you can move on to what you need to feel financially secure after the divorce. You may be in a divorce situation where you need assets, or you may be in one where you need to secure more retirement money. Based on your debts, your best-case scenario could be to leave the marriage with manageable debt. As I said, you cannot get in divorce what you don't already have. You cannot give in divorce what you don't already have. If you follow the math and the money, you can make informed decisions about what you need

> *"Everyone hates a vicious animal. Don't hire one as your divorce attorney."*

—ANTONIA ROYBAL-MACK

CHAPTER 5
Avoid the Bulldogs

The most critical decision that you will make in this divorce is who you choose to advocate for you. It may determine your overall outcome. It may determine any hope of leaving on good terms with your soon-to-be ex and remaining friends. It will certainly determine your stress level in this process and the financial cost of the decision to divorce. You need to find a lawyer that is competent and has technical skills. You do not need an unstable person guiding this ship. You will have your own crazy to manage in this process. How do you prepare for the fight of your life when you're already feeling defeated? Key one: You get a good gladiator on your side, one that does not look like a rabid animal.

THE MOST CRITICAL DECISION THAT YOU WILL MAKE IN THIS DIVORCE IS WHO YOU CHOOSE TO ADVOCATE FOR YOU.

A bulldog attorney looks like Cruella de Vil, and not the Emma Stone Cruella, but the Glenn Close version. Her voice sounds like nails on a chalkboard. She is vicious and her words can cut like a knife. It is certain that her words will make getting your case resolved in mediation unlikely, because the other side will have no choice but to protect themselves from her fire. She will be unprepared in court and will provide exhibits that are full of shock and awe but will be unhelpful to the judge in helping decide your case. The bulldog cannot be wrong, so she will continue to slash away at your spouse, eventually causing you, your case, and any hope of a positive relationship in the future with your ex to be impossibly ruined.

The one question you never want to ask when interviewing a divorce lawyer is "Are you a bulldog?" When I am asked that question, it is an immediate sign not to take a case. I know that you may want to feel protected and feel that aggression is necessary. You may want to inflict harm on the person that you just decided ruined your life. But this is not what you want in a lawyer. Usually, if I am asked that question, I will end the intake and let the person know that I am not the right lawyer for their case. I'll try to educate the client that if they are looking for a bulldog, they are starting the process looking for the wrong thing. The legal process is not where you go to find fairness. You cannot spend justice, and it does not help you sleep at night.

THE LEGAL PROCESS IS NOT WHERE YOU GO TO FIND FAIRNESS.

LOOK FOR A LEVEL HEAD

There are no winners or losers in family court. The process is stressful, expensive, and not where to search for your future values. If you want vindication or to feel right, then go get a Magic 8 Ball; don't use the court process for that. It will cost too much and leave you feeling empty. The court process is designed to divide money and look after children. It has no other purpose. It is not meant to provide a space for fighting, yet it is the most combative place in the courthouse.

In choosing a lawyer, you need to know that emotion and intellect work inversely. When emotion goes up, intellect goes down. That means that if your lawyer is sitting crying with you or angry and emotional during the process, their intellect is not working for you. If your lawyer is angry in court or acting like a bulldog, they are not thinking clearly enough to help you. Now, I'm ruthless in defending my clients, but I do it without being vile. There is a process, a professionalism, and a way to get results without my client being punished.

TRAPS TO AVOID

There are a few traps to avoid in hiring a lawyer:

- The good marketing trap
- The advocate-at-all-costs trap
- The job skipper trap

THE GOOD MARKETING TRAP

Just because a lawyer has a great commercial does not mean they are a good lawyer—it means they have a good marketing company. More accurate are online reviews, things written about the lawyer in the local newspaper, or awards given by the local bar association.

> JUST BECAUSE A LAWYER HAS A GREAT COMMERCIAL DOES NOT MEAN THEY ARE A GOOD LAWYER—IT MEANS THEY HAVE A GOOD MARKETING COMPANY.

When you're searching for a lawyer, look at the middle of the online reviews, not the five-star ratings. Those reviews are likely from the marketing company. Also, ignore the one-star reviews, because there are people who love to troll Google and give nasty reviews to everyone. There are some people that cannot be happy at Disneyland. The middle-of-the-road reviews will give the most honest feedback.

The Who's Who or Super Lawyers list is nothing more than a paid advertisement by that lawyer, so avoid those, as well as top lawyer rankings—it's all paid advertising. If the lawyer you're researching has received awards from local entities and bar associations, then those are reputable. I have seen so many commercials for terrible lawyers that I wouldn't trust to tie my shoes correctly, and yet they have clients because people do not know how to research them. Good marketing has worked for Nike, and lawyers do the same thing. However, if your Nikes suck, you are out $100. If your lawyer sucks, you might be left with only $100.

THE ADVOCATE-AT-ALL-COSTS TRAP

The advocate-at-all-costs lawyer knows they cannot win, and they see you coming with an open checkbook. This lawyer will falsely tell you that you can win (even though you can't) and will create conflict to keep you in court. If a lawyer is creating more conflict in your life rather than less, then they are the wrong lawyer for you.

Here are some phrases this type of lawyer might use:

- "If your ex wasn't such a deadbeat . . . "
- "If that guy wasn't such a loser . . . "

The language these lawyers use drives conflict rather than resolving it. Even worse, this lawyer talks this way in front of your ex and in front of the judge. You should know that judges do not like nasty lawyers. They like lawyers that are competent, realistic, and scrupulous.

THE JOB SKIPPER TRAP

If a lawyer has worked for a lot of law firms within a short period of time, then there are issues that you should be aware of. Each time a lawyer moves or shifts, it will affect your case. If the lawyer you're working with leaves, you might be bounced to a new lawyer, and it takes time and money to get that next lawyer up to speed on your case. You definitely don't want to work with a lawyer that has a reputation for firm jumping. Also, if the law firm has a history of lawyers leaving constantly, then it's an issue. Looking on LinkedIn or doing a simple Google search will give you this information.

LAWS ARE PRACTICAL; EMOTIONS ARE NOT

Here is a hint: Divorce laws are just that . . . laws. They are written down with specificity. Someone in your legislature, over the course of hundreds of years, has codified this stuff. Committees sat there over time and determined what the word "income" means in divorce. They figured out how things are divided, what is joint or community property, what is separate property, and generally who gets what. Some committee 20 years ago sat and decided a formula for child support and a formula for spousal support.

There is not a single place in the law that says, "The most emotional person wins." You will never find a case that states, "The bitchiest and meanest lawyer wins." The inverse is true. The person that understands the rules and understands how those rules apply to your facts will win. More importantly, a good lawyer will tell you when you are going to lose and when you need to choose a different path. If someone comes to me and says, "I want $15,000 a month in spousal support" or "I want to pay only $1,000 in spousal support," I'll tell them what's realistic. Both of those asks are extreme and it's the lawyer's job to say, "That goal is unrealistic."

YOU WILL NEVER FIND A CASE THAT STATES, "THE BITCHIEST AND MEANEST LAWYER WINS."

There are lawyers in our town who will crusade for their client all the way to trial, even when we all know that they can't win. Oftentimes, those lawyers end up paying my attorney's fees, because they never tell their client that what they are asking for is a fantasy not supported by the law. Even worse, after stringing along the client all the way to trial, they will dismiss all the motions the morning of trial.

Choosing a lawyer to guide you through this process is a big investment. That investment should not leave you empty-handed when you leave the courtroom. Every dollar that you spend on attorney's fees is one dollar less for your future. Therefore—this point is critical—you need to know that *drama always costs money*. If you want a pound of flesh, the courts are not the place to get it. You are in this process for one end: a divorce. If you want vindication or peace, this is not the place to find it. You need to find a lawyer that is not going to try to deliver vindication. If your lawyer does not outline risk for you or tell you when you are wrong, then they are not doing their job. The lawyer is not the hero in this process but rather the guide.

When your lawyer tells you what your possible outcome might be, you need to ask:

- What is the upside?
- What is the downside?
- Can I live with the downside?

Now, if you're thinking, "But my ex is savvy and a liar. I need someone that is going to fight back." That's not true. No matter how savvy they are, they are not above the law. You need someone who knows the law, knows the rules, and can apply your facts to the rules. You need someone that is going to understand all of your holdings and how the law divides each one. You need someone that understands a bargain when they see it and will tell you to end the case when the time and offer is right.

YOU NEED SOMEONE THAT UNDERSTANDS A BARGAIN WHEN THEY SEE IT AND WILL TELL YOU TO END THE CASE WHEN THE TIME AND OFFER IS RIGHT.

Client Story

The Blood Seeker

I have had countless cases where my client wanted blood and they would have paid me to continue a case that didn't need to be dragged out so that they could get exactly that.

There was one case in particular in which my client wanted to go to trial just to "see what happens." My fee would have easily been

$100,000 for that trial, which was dissolving a 40-year marriage with multiple businesses.

This client had built these businesses because she wasn't afraid of a little risk. It was my job to tell her and educate her that the risk of going forward and not settling outweighed the reward. I had to tell her that I did not believe that she could do better at trial. That meant that I walked away from a large fee, but I knew it was right for her to settle.

If you were headed into surgery, would you want an emotional doctor that was "feeling your pain"? Would you want a doctor that was going to commiserate with you in your fear? Would you want a doctor that was going to cry with you when you talk about how unfair it is that you have to deal with this medical condition when, after all, you didn't ask for it? Not likely. You want a doctor that is going to walk into surgery calm and confident; one who will tell you what their process is to get you safely in and out of surgery. The doctor will tell you the risks of the surgery with confidence and certainty, and then explain why the benefits of the surgery outweigh the risks. The doctor is not going to have a big ego and say, "I am (fill-in-the-blank law school) trained, and you need to listen to me." Instead, a good surgeon is going to walk you through, and with their technical skills get you to the other side of, surgery.

You want nothing less in a lawyer. You are looking for technical skill. You are looking for someone who will tell you if you are wrong. You want someone to educate you on the risks and the rewards, and that can tell you when something is going to sting, even just a little. Any lawyer that guarantees you a result should not be trusted. Any lawyer that promises that the other side will suffer is lying.

YOU WANT A LAWYER TO EDUCATE YOU ON THE RISKS AND THE REWARDS, AND TELL YOU WHEN SOMETHING IS GOING TO STING, EVEN JUST A LITTLE.

So, you ask, how do you hire the right lawyer? You research them. Depending on the complexity of your case, the cost to bring them on board may be anywhere from a used car to a nice house. You would never buy either without doing your research.

If your case is of high enough value, go watch the lawyer in court. Also, follow your instincts. Law firms are businesses. Businesses have to engage in marketing to stay in business. Thus, law firms hire marketing people and professional copywriters to advance their online presence. This means: Do not trust only what you see online. You need to meet with people and ask friends for a referral. Most importantly: Trust your instincts. If you do not feel good about the person or their approach, walk away, and interview more lawyers until you find one that you trust.

Here are some questions to ask your lawyer:

1. How long have you been practicing?

2. Have you handled a case like mine before?

3. Do you have the time to dedicate to my case?

4. How are your fees handled?

5. What is the retainer?

6. Do you anticipate handing this work off to a junior lawyer? If so, how do you supervise the junior lawyer?

7. Are my goals realistic?

8. What will you need from me to evaluate if my goals are realistic?

9. What kind of time will you need from me to prepare the case?

10. How do you keep drama out of the process?

11. How will we prepare together before each step in the process?

12. If my case does not settle outside of court, are you willing to take it to trial?

13. Can you be aggressive in preparing my case without being nasty in court?

Follow your instincts and hire the person that sits well with you, the person that is going to get this handled so that you can return to regular life.

MEAN LAWYERS COST MONEY

I have never done a divorce where the marriage did not start based upon love or something that looked like love. At the end of your case, especially if you have children, you want to be able to be in a room with your ex. It might not be immediately, and it might take time, but if you hire a lawyer that is going to be nasty for no purpose except to be nasty, then you lose all hope for peace in the future. You don't walk into a stranger's house to pet their vicious bulldog—why would you walk into a courtroom with one? If you hire a mean lawyer, it will not render you a better result and it will cost more money. Lawyers can be aggressive in getting information and preparation, but it doesn't serve you in front of the judge.

> AT THE END OF YOUR CASE, ESPECIALLY
> IF YOU HAVE CHILDREN, YOU WANT TO BE
> ABLE TO BE IN A ROOM WITH YOUR EX.

THE POWER OF WORDS

Justice is based on the words that you use. Words matter in this venue. Make this a fundamental part of your defense. Words said in court cannot be taken back. If you have children, know that. Keep in mind that the opposing party has seen you at your worst. He or she has known you and witnessed times when the wheels fell off. He or she is privy to the one night you got too sad and drank too much. He has witnessed the secret parts of you that you don't want the world to see. On the converse, you have seen the same. You have witnessed every poor decision and bad act. If you're going to blame your ex for the bad, blame effectively—and blame them for the good as well.

During this process, you will need to share intimate details with your lawyer. You don't want to embarrass your ex-spouse—you want to get divorced—so be sure to hire someone that can make that happen with as little drama as possible.

Losing Big with a Bulldog

I had a case where my client was exceptionally reasonable. She wanted something very simple. She wanted her ex-wife—who along with their child was being abused by her current spouse—to get some help and keep the child away from the abuser. She didn't want to eradicate the mother, which was her right in light of what the child had experienced at the hands of the stepparent, and in light of the mother knowing about it and doing nothing. The other mom hired a bulldog.

In court, the bulldog was nasty and foaming at the mouth. She told my client that her concerns were nothing more than a "custody grab" and something completely fabricated by my client. She argued that the child had "atrocious table manners, she slurps her food, chews with her mouth open, and, your honor, is just a little slob." These were her words to explain to the judge why the child was abused. It wasn't until Child Protective Services testified, that Mom saw that she was going to lose—and lose big—with this bulldog.

I was called the day after the hearing, and even though the bulldog was still calling the child a slob, she did offer to settle. However, my client wouldn't have it. She wanted to go for the jugular by that point. She was ready to spend anything to prove that their child was not a slob—because bulldogs make you want to protect yourself, even if they are going to lose. I gave her the lesson on bulldogs, we settled the case, and the child was protected.

In hiring a lawyer, be clear about your expectations. Be clear about what you need them to accomplish. Ask them to tell you when you are wrong. Ask them to be there to walk you through the process, step by step, as the guide. Find someone that you can trust. Above all, follow your intuition—it is not wrong.

"A goal without a plan is nothing more than a wish."

—ANTOINE DE SAINT-EXUPÉRY

CHAPTER 6

Know Your Outcome

I f there is one chapter where you truly should heed my advice, it's this one: Know your outcome.

This chapter might make your head spin. However, if there is one chapter that can help guide you to your future, it is this one. You cannot shoot darts in the dark and expect the bullseye. You have to know what you're aiming for. I cannot stress that enough.

YOU CANNOT SHOOT DARTS IN THE DARK AND EXPECT THE BULLSEYE. YOU HAVE TO KNOW WHAT YOU'RE AIMING FOR.

Imagine that the darts that you're throwing at that bullseye cost $1,000 each. How insane would it be to blindly throw them at the board? Now your divorce is the dart game and it costs money, so you'd better have the lights on, your eyes open, and your focus on the target.

There are times as mothers—working mothers, busy mothers—that we see that dreaded text message from school reminding us of the parent/teacher potluck tonight and that cupcakes are needed at 5:30 p.m. sharp. If you are like me, if that email did not hit my assistant's inbox, the potluck was not on the calendar, and the cupcakes were nowhere on my radar. How is the problem solved? Simple: I race to the nearest grocery store, run inside, grab the nearest cupcakes, and head to the meeting. It is simple. In that moment, I know my outcome. My outcome is to get the cupcakes and get to the meeting. Divorce is no different.

I know it sounds ludicrous that divorce is as simple as arriving at a pot-luck with the promised dessert, but the ideas are the same: Know your outcome. When you know your outcome, you can walk in, get what you want, only spend what you need to spend, and you're done.

We have all had the opposite trip. On a Sunday afternoon, we head to the nearest Costco to pick up laundry soap or some other mundane item from the big-box store. When we walk inside, we don't walk straight to the laundry section in the far-right corner. Instead, we turn left and walk aisle by aisle until our cart is full before we ever get to the detergent. This endeavor takes twice as long and is 10 times more expensive. The divorce process can be the same way. Nothing of extreme value in the cart, but it was really expensive to get there.

THE DIVORCE PROCESS CAN BE THE SAME WAY. NOTHING OF EXTREME VALUE IN THE CART, BUT IT WAS REALLY EXPENSIVE TO GET THERE.

In this example, it is easy to respond, "I don't know what I want, so how can I walk into the store and get just that? I need to look around to know what I want." Fair. But I will guide you to look around much faster. You have already done the exercises to understand what you own and what you owe. Now, let me guide you on knowing which items on the ledger need to end up in your column at the end of the case.

In knowing your outcome, don't look for fairness. Start by looking for what you need. Imagine if your soon-to-be-ex-spouse did the same thing and shared with you what they wanted. Imagine if this divorce process was not a chess game but instead a poker game with all the cards faceup. Not all cases can be that way, but if yours has the possibility, explore it.

THE TARGET

Imagine going to the shooting range for a competition. You stand in your cubicle with your firearm loaded and you look downrange. However, there is no target, just a 200-yard stretch with nothing at the end but a dirt hill. Where do you aim? How do you know if you hit the mark? How do you know if you are a winner or loser without a target?

Think about your divorce outcome like a target. The inner ring is what you need and you cannot live without. The next ring is what you need but you can live without. The ring outside of that is what you want but you do not need. The outer ring is the fluff. The metaphorical fluff—if you get it in the divorce, it would be enjoyable.

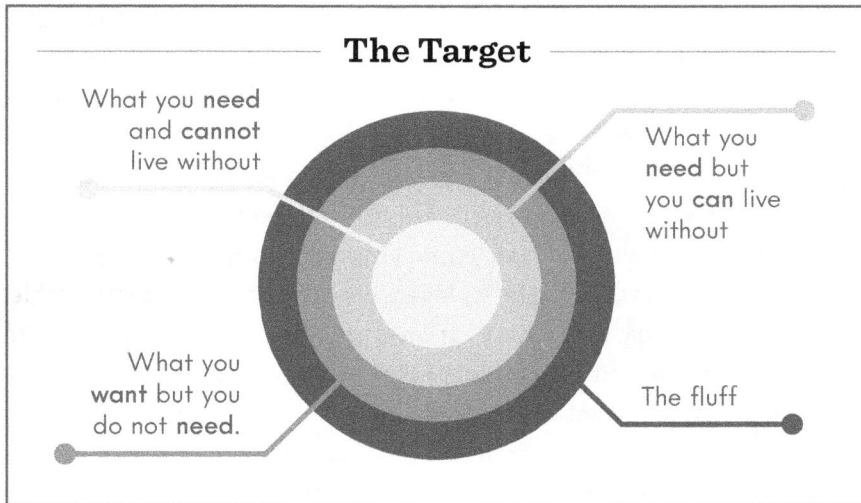

The Target

What you **need** and **cannot** live without

What you **need** but you **can** live without

What you **want** but you do not **need**.

The fluff

If you walk into your lawyer's office with just a range down yonder and not a clear picture of what you want, it will be more emotional and costly than necessary. Therefore, take the picture of the target at the back of the book and get clear on what you need, what you want, and what is just fluff.

YOUR OUTCOME BUCKETS

Another way to think about defining your outcome is to put your needs and desires in separate buckets.

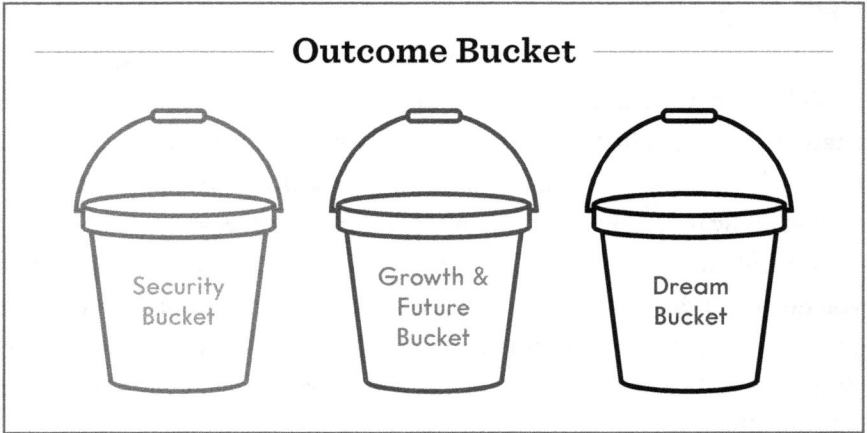

Outcome Bucket

Security Bucket

Growth & Future Bucket

Dream Bucket

The first bucket is the security bucket. Again, this is everything that you absolutely need to provide a safe and healthy home for yourself and your children (if applicable). This bucket is the same as the inner ring of your bullseye—it's for must-haves.

An example of something that would go here is suitable housing. If you are accustomed to living in a residence in a gated community, then suitable housing would not be an apartment in an undesirable neighborhood. Suitable housing is going to be a place where you feel safe, comfortable, and not like you "lost everything." It's a place where you can stay going to the same gym and your kids remain in the same school.

In the security bucket, things are not lavish but instead secure and safe. This might be moving from the large house by the country club to a townhome in the adjacent gated community. It is still safe, it is still secure, but it's not accompanied by the prestigious address.

IN THE SECURITY BUCKET, THINGS ARE NOT LAVISH BUT INSTEAD SECURE AND SAFE.

The inner ring of the bullseyes includes cash on hand. If your estate has cash within it, you will want some of that cash as a safety net. The inner ring and security bucket includes health insurance and access to healthcare, a reliable vehicle, and insurance for your belongings. Depending on your age, your retirement accounts might be in this bucket. In this space, put the basic necessities of life that you must have. Your luxurious, overpriced face cream does not go into this bucket. If you woke up the morning after your divorce with the items in the security bucket, then you can grow from there. If you have these items, then you are financially whole.

The second bucket, or next ring, is the growth and future bucket. The future bucket is to set you up for the future. This includes offloading debilitating debt that will prevent your future from being successful. Again, depending on your age, this would include your retirement accounts, whole-life insurance policies, luxury vehicles, or purchasing a similar home in size and location. This includes continued private school for your children and the ability to continue to drive the Range Rover. This bucket includes investment accounts, cryptocurrency accounts, and the things that you will need to start growing a future. If you own a business, your business goes into the future bucket—unless it is your sole source of income, in which case it stays in the security bucket.

THE FUTURE BUCKET IS TO SET YOU UP FOR THE FUTURE. THIS INCLUDES OFFLOADING DEBILITATING DEBT THAT WILL PREVENT YOUR FUTURE FROM BEING SUCCESSFUL.

In some divorces, the marital estate does not have sufficient funds to have anything in the future bucket. Unfortunately, if you were living on the fringes before the divorce, you will eventually take out some of your security bucket assets and start to fill the growth and future bucket.

The third and final bucket is the dream bucket, or the outer ring. These are the items that you will take because you can, not because you need them or want them. These are the second homes, the luxury vehicles, the boat, the RV, the third big screen from the second bedroom, the entire cryptocurrency account, etc. These are the items that have value, but if you do not get them, your life will not be materially altered.

A key example that was so apparent during the pandemic was designer clothing, purses, and shoes. These have value to you, they were expensive to purchase, but then the pandemic hit. You had nowhere to wear those beautiful things. I mean, you and your Louis Vuitton could flaunt around the living room, but there was no need for luggage in a world that was not boarding a plane. Think of this bucket as all those things in the pandemic that lost all value—the season tickets to the concert venue, sports team, and opera are in this bucket. The clothing worn to charity art events lives here.

As a nation, so many people used the pandemic to get perspective on what was important to them. For me, I used a luxury dry cleaner and regularly purchased new business suits and jewelry. In New Mexico, we have the best Native American jewelry in the world. For holidays and birthdays, my husband would gift me with the best and most beautiful trinkets. The pandemic hit, courts closed, and I had nowhere to wear these items. I have not purchased a new suit since the pandemic, because I had so many and I went at least 14 months without needing a single one. The jewelry has no value if I cannot wear it. Think of this outer ring and bucket the same way. The outer ring includes all the things that you set aside during the pandemic because you simply did not need them. Depending on where you lived in the country, you had various degrees of this. I was in the state with the strictest COVID restrictions, so I needed nothing but a roof over my head, groceries in my fridge, and a solid Wi-Fi connection to survive.

THE OUTER RING INCLUDES ALL THE THINGS THAT YOU SET ASIDE DURING THE PANDEMIC BECAUSE YOU SIMPLY DID NOT NEED THEM.

As a culture, we are so hooked on instant gratification that we don't understand the beauty and patience of taking baby steps in the right direction. Ego and revenge have no place here. When you write out your goals for your divorce outcomes, be specific about what you want. If your list is based on revenge, you're not likely to be happy in the end either way. You cannot base your lists on what you think you can have or what your spouse will do. This exercise has nothing to do with what your spouse will agree to; this exercise is not about chess. This exercise is about what you need to start tomorrow. That is not license to be unrealistic, but license to write down your own personal goals for the first time.

As part of the exercise, you need to be realistic about debt and spousal support. Whether you are going to be the payer or payee of spousal support, be sure to include spousal support and child support in the security bucket. Be sure to include a monthly budget of what you actually need to survive after the divorce. If you have never done a budget, go online, Google "budget template," and get to work.

Even if you have enough assets to comfortably remain in the dream bucket all the time, you will need a budget. If you do not have a budget, you do not have a target. Even Melinda Gates lost half her wealth in divorce. You must think in those terms now.

SMART GOALS

Now that you have a framework to start deciding what you need to be secure, grow, and dream, you might still feel some hesitation about filling in the buckets. What if you make a mistake, what if you are wrong? As mothers and women, our human instincts have one simple mission: Prevent our young from starving and get them to adulthood so that humanity can continue. That raw instinct makes second-guessing a lot more involved than it needs to be. First, if you have the security bucket, your young will not starve. More importantly, we live in the most abundant nation on Earth, so when those thoughts come up, recognize them as ancient and dismiss them. We will take a deeper dive later to answer more questions.

WHAT IS YOUR GOAL?

You now know that you need to have a specific goal or outcome. It cannot just be "I want a divorce." In many of my initial intakes with clients, they say that all they want is freedom. This makes sense because leaving a marriage naturally puts you in fight or flight mode. When you are in fight of flight mode, your brain wants one thing and that is to end the stimulus that caused the fight or flight reaction. That means leaving, running, just getting divorced, and leaving it all behind. It means that you will do anything, sign anything, even if it's bad for you, just to have this over. However, once you get to the other side of the divorce fight or flight, if you do not have a clear outcome, you are not secure and will experience fight or flight all over again—only this time it will be for basic survival.

WHEN YOU ARE IN FIGHT OR FLIGHT MODE, YOUR BRAIN WANTS ONE THING AND THAT IS TO END THE STIMULUS THAT CAUSE THE FIGHT OR FLIGHT.

In most of these 50 United States, if you ask the court for a divorce, the minimum outcome is that you will eventually be granted a divorce. So your outcome needs to be stated specifically and put in writing. Then you need to write the steps needed to get there and they need to be stated for ONLY yourself. Here is a framework that you can use.

1. What is the goal or outcome?
2. State each goal in the positive, not the negative. This is an exercise in what you want, not what you do not want.
   a. Stated in the positive: I want to keep the house.
   b. State in the negative: I do not want to lose the house.
   c. Trust me, these brain gymnastics in this process will save you money and help you stay focused on what you need.
3. Can you state it specifically?
4. Is there a time frame involved to achieve the goal?
5. What steps are needed to get there?
6. Is it measurable?

7. Is it stated for yourself only? Your highest purpose and outcome?

After this exercise, your outcome should look something like this:

1. My outcome is to leave this relationship in peace with a three-bedroom house in a safe neighborhood with under $30,000 in debt and the ability to meet my monthly budget with my own current income. (Think solely about your future, because you will spend all of your time there.)

2. My specific outcome is to keep my house with a mortgage that I can pay off in five years, to have a working vehicle that will not need to be replaced for three or more years, and to be able to maintain my weekly personal care appointments.

3. I want to achieve this goal within the next two weeks to two years. (Ask your lawyer what a realistic time is in your state for both a contested and uncontested divorce. But do put a time frame on it.)

4. I need to take the following steps to get there:

   a. Create a detailed budget with current expenses.

   b. Created a detailed budget with future expenses.

   c. Study the ledgers created in the Joneses chapter to get a clear picture of my finances.

   d. Engage a therapist or coach.

   e. Engage an attorney.

   f. Meet with a financial planner (even if you only have debt).

   g. Talk to a mortgage broker to understand your credit.

While preparing this list, write EVERYTHING down that comes into your head. It can be repetitive. We will make it manageable later. There are no wrong or silly answers. If it comes into your head, write it down.

Next, decide how you will know when you have closure on this goal.

Is it when your ex signs the papers? When the judge signs the papers? When you move into your new place? It can be anything that is measurable and meaningful to you.

Finally, is this goal just for you? For this goal only, I will allow you to include your children. This means that you can add what your kids would need to feel whole and secure after this process. For example, in my house, birthdays are national holidays, i.e., a big deal. It takes money to host a holiday; therefore, I need to set money aside for those events. Frivolous? Yes. Important to me? Yes.

If you focused on all of the steps that it took to do anything meaningful in your life, you probably would have never started. You cannot focus on the steps that it will take to reach your outcome; instead, focus on why you want it and what you will feel when you achieve it. You can take any task and turn it into a million little things, or you can make it one thing. For example, you decide that you want to stop at the salon on the way home. You can take that from "I need to download the app, log in to my email to verify my email address, make an appointment, confirm the appointment via text message, leave work early, drive to the appointment, find parking, pay the parking garage, walk to the salon, check in, answer the COVID questionnaire, wait in the guest area, then get my hair washed and dried." Walking through the steps to get your hair done is overwhelming! Instead of listing each thing that must be done to accomplish that very simple goal, turn all of these tasks into one statement: "I am going to the salon after work." If you think of each task that it takes to get your hair done, you might just say, "Naw, not today." Deciding what you want from your divorce is no different. Most of us would never get out of bed in the morning if we knew all of the tasks that needed to be completed in each day. Instead, when we focus on the outcomes, there is a different experience. Now, does it mean that the tasks are ignored and do not need to get done? Not a chance. It just means we're reframing it.

IF YOU FOCUSED ON ALL OF THE STEPS THAT IT TOOK TO DO ANYTHING MEANINGFUL IN YOUR LIFE, YOU PROBABLY WOULD HAVE NEVER STARTED.

Go back to the early days of brainstorming sessions with everything in its own bubble. (Side note: Thank heavens those ended 20 years ago.) Let's revive this archaic technique for this exercise only. Put all category to-dos together. For example, if you need to sell your house, selling the house, buying a new one, and calling movers can all go into the Real Estate Agent category.

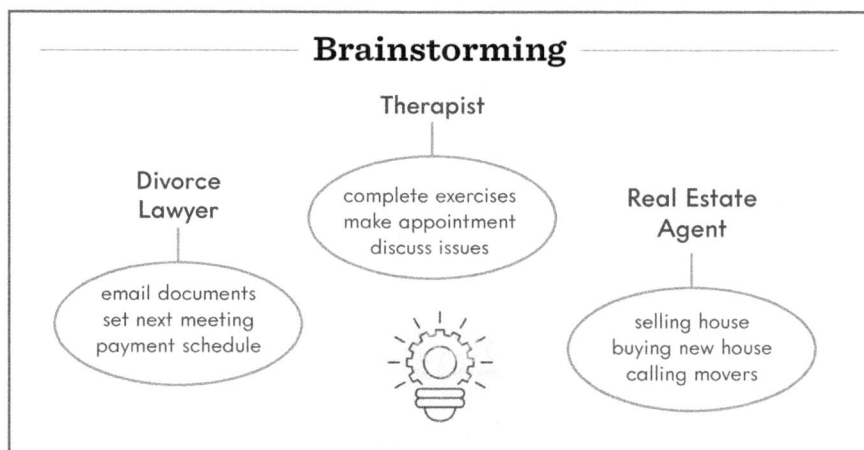

Brainstorming

Therapist
- complete exercises
- make appointment
- discuss issues

Divorce Lawyer
- email documents
- set next meeting
- payment schedule

Real Estate Agent
- selling house
- buying new house
- calling movers

Once you put like items together, decide what you need to do, what needs to be assigned to your divorce lawyer, what needs to be assigned to your therapist, and what things do not actually need to be done at all. Then take action. Send individual emails to your lawyer, your assistant, your therapist, and whoever else is necessary to accomplish this list. Then get it scheduled and get it done.

You have been broken down before. You have set goals and then life has completely derailed them—maybe a car accident delayed boarding the plane on your dream vacation. Divorce is no different.

YOU HAVE SET GOALS AND THEN LIFE
HAS COMPLETELY DERAILED THEM—MAYBE
A CAR ACCIDENT DELAYED BOARDING
THE PLANE ON YOUR DREAM VACATION.
DIVORCE IS NO DIFFERENT.

Is this a perfect world? No. Are you going to get everything on that goal list? Probably not. But you can focus on what is possible, rather than what is impossible. This might be the most important point in setting your outcome.

WHAT ARE YOUR LIMITING BELIEFS?

It's time to look at your limiting beliefs to determine if they're getting in the way of getting what you actually want. For example, say that you want your ex's 401(k). You yourself are five years away from retirement and you have cashed out yours over the years for everything from vacations to the new hot tub in a residence that sold three years ago. However, you don't want to ask for the 401(k) because he would never give it to you. Now, if you do not get sufficient retirement assets in the divorce, you have resigned yourself to working years beyond your desired mark. In this scenario, what you want has real leverage on your life right now and your life in the future. A limiting belief—one that says "There's no way I'll ask for that 401(k), let alone get it"—puts you at a huge disadvantage.

Remember, divorce is only about the future, the place you will spend the rest of your days. So if you are afraid to ask, then ask yourself these questions first:

- What would happen if you did?

- What wouldn't happen if you did?

- What would happen if you didn't?

- What wouldn't happen if you didn't?

That twisted you up, I know. So now that I have your attention: Ask for what you want, even if you think you cannot have it or you have already lost it and will never have it again. If you allow your limiting beliefs to get in the way here, then you will get less than what you want and may not even end up with what you need.

You don't get what you want in life. You get what you ask for.

YOU DON'T GET WHAT YOU WANT IN LIFE. YOU GET WHAT YOU ASK FOR.

Good things do not come to those who wait, and smart girls are not the quiet girls. You do not get more when you are seen and not heard. You cannot wait for things to come to you. You must go out, seek them, and get them.

Now that you know where you are, and you have set some goals to define where you are going, it's time to talk about how to get there. You need to become a master negotiator for what you want. Being a master negotiator does not mean that you ask for the moon and hope that you land in the stars. That is nothing more than a dumb motivational saying on a T-shirt. A master negotiator knows the outcome that they are looking for and how to start just high enough to get an agreement. If you are passively reading this book or listening on Audible while driving home, stop now. Don't let your financial audit go unwritten. Don't let your goals and outcomes go unwritten. Neither I nor any other lawyer can help you if you do not help yourself. It's time to come to your own rescue. I cannot help you learn to negotiate and get in a framework to negotiate if you do not know where you are and where you are going.

NEITHER I NOR ANY OTHER LAWYER CAN HELP YOU IF YOU DO NOT HELP YOURSELF. IT'S TIME TO COME TO YOUR OWN RESCUE.

Once I worked with a lawyer who was very fond of himself and his capabilities. During the negotiation, he said, "Look, we have come down 90 percent and you have only moved 10 percent," in an effort to get my client to move in his direction. I reminded him that we were always playing with real money on our side of the table and that they were playing with fantasy money, so the 10 percent where we lived was real life. Good negotiators are realistic. So be a good negotiator

---

Client Story
The Negotiator

Once of the best negotiators that I have ever known was an elderly client of mine. This woman had built an empire from hard work in an industry that did not advance women at the time she was rising in it. I was so grateful to be her lawyer, because I knew that my learnings in the case would be substantial.

In negotiating the final outcome, she was very clear on day one about what she wanted. For this client, priority number one was getting a piece of real estate that had been in the family and had a certain sentimental value to her. She wanted this above all else.

As the case went on, this outcome remained her only focus. On day 600, with the case delayed by COVID, she was still very clear on what she wanted and it was exactly the same as day one. Because she was so clear on the outcome, I had advance warning to prepare a case to get her that outcome.

With every offer that came across the table, she said no, until it was exactly what she wanted. By that time, the facts had been established, the law was in her favor, and she was confident that she could get a yes in court if needed. In negotiation, we reached an agreement that was exactly what she wanted. The outcome to begin with was reasonable. However, the following morning, the other side decided to back out. Her response? "Do what you have to do with any means necessary, so long as it is legal and gets me my outcome."

We went to work. Within 30 days, the other side knew that she was steadfast, and they signed the original paperwork. One interesting thing was that, at the start of the case, she was incredibly clear on what she wanted. Then she had been telling the other side in simplistic terms what she wanted. It took both sides a great deal of money, motions practice, and back-and-forth, and she got what she wanted. She was right to begin with. If the other side had seen that, they would have saved a great deal of money and 600 days.

In negotiating, knowing what you want is not a tool to hurt the other person, to show them what they left, or to show them how far you have come in finding your power. This is a time to decide what you can live with to buy you freedom and peace. In sad cases, you may also have to buy your kids. It is not the time to "get it all" but instead the time to get what you need. It's also the most important time to be realistic and listen to the professionals around you.

IT IS NOT THE TIME TO "GET IT ALL" BUT INSTEAD THE TIME TO GET WHAT YOU NEED.

Before you start any negotiation toward your goals, ask yourself:

1. Are you negotiating with the right person?

   a. This sounds simple, but if you want the lake cabin that his parents are also attached to, does your spouse really have the ability to make the decision? If you know that your ex-monster-in-law really wants time with the kids during the holidays and is the one paying the legal bills, ask who needs to be in the room so that a decision can be made. I often have clients get furious when their ex brings their new fling, sister, or mother to the negotiation, yet if those people are influencing your ex and their decisions, they need to be in the room. It is not just your spouse that you are negotiating with. If your spouse is relying on their parents, best friend, sister, and priest, and they are the decision makers, then they need to be in the room.

    b. You need anyone in the room who has the ability to make the decision.

2. Is the other person willing to arrive at an agreement?

    a. Again, it seems simple enough, but most divorces settle in two places. The first is right in what we call the sweet spot of the divorce where neither party wants to hurt the other; they just want out. That is a great place to make an agreement, because both parties are willing to come to an agreement. The remainder settle when both spouses are finally ready—emotionally ready—to arrive at an agreement and have such litigation fatigue that they just want it over. They don't want to send another payment to their lawyer, expert, or mediator, and it just needs to end. Try to settle before you get to that point. A small percentage of cases never settle and are decided by a judge. If your spouse does not want to reach an agreement, wants to see you suffer, see you spend money, or just see you in person again, even if it is in court, then negotiation may not work. Both sides need to want to reach an agreement.

3. Can you find the first common agreement, no matter how small the agreement?

    a. If you both agree that the other loves your children, you've got a starting point. You don't have to agree on the definition of love, just know that you both love them. If you can, find the simplest and smallest area for agreement. Another might be that you both agree that this process has been expensive, you both agree that the process has been hard, etc. Find something to agree on, anything, then move from there. You can even agree on the fact that you can't stand each other and need to end the misery. Just find an agreement.

4. Where are the places of conflict?

a. Discover the positions of each of the parts in conflict and get to work. Push beyond your boundaries and only make agreements on the way down the list that are in alignment with your goals. Go from the largest agreement in three and move down the list as slowly as you can continue to agree. During this process, continue to remind yourself of your intention in getting to a resolution. Ask yourself over and over what your intention is until you are clear. Be open to all of the different ways to find a resolution. You may not have thought of selling the summer cabin and just buying a new one. You may not have thought of all the creative ways to pay off debt. Then move toward agreement. Cases are always best resolved in mediation because you can control your outcome instead of letting a judge decide what is best for your life. You may have to move, but if you know your outcome and you know what you need in that security bucket, you can find flexible ways to get it. On the flip side of that coin, if you feel pushed into something that you cannot live with, or the security bucket is getting sparse, then you can say "no."

HOW TO MAKE NEGOTIATION EASIER

There are some things that makes this process easier.

First and foremost, hire the best professionals and mediator that you can afford. Mediators are the go-between. They are professional messengers that are often the first go-to when couples cannot agree before they go to court. Research your mediator and realize that the best mediators are probably the most expensive. Experience matters in selecting your mediator. As a lawyer, I have to trust the mediator's opinion before

I will tell my client to trust them. That means the mediator should have done more cases than me through trial. Good mediators do not get there with a weekend class on consensus. They get there after spending years as judges, lawyers, accountants, or the highest-level professional in their fields. They become mediators after being the best.

FIRST AND FOREMOST, HIRE THE BEST PROFESSIONALS AND MEDIATOR THAT YOU CAN AFFORD.

I will not use a mediator that I regularly litigate against or face in court. Why? Because if I think I can beat them and that they are wrong, I will not trust them as the guide. Like many lawyers, I have settled more cases in mediation than at trial. What is important is that you have a lawyer that is willing to go to trial if the process breaks down.

I have had clients that don't get everything that they want in mediation, but you are always negotiating against the backdrop of: Is this realistic? Can I do better in front of a judge? You know to settle when the answers to those questions are yes and no, respectively. Also, if your ex is a gaslighter and complete jerk, just stay focused, and this is where you use what you know about them to get your result. If they are significance-driven, give them the depreciating sports car so you can have the retirement accounts. It's all just a means to get the right assets in the right column on the ledger.

At each stage in the mediation and negotiation process, go back to the questions listed in the prior chapter.

1. What is the upside?

2. What is the downside?

3. Can I live with the downside?

Will this be perfect? If you ride off into the sunset on your private jet, maybe. Maybe right now, maybe in the future. I have seen so many clients get their outcomes even after divorce. They couldn't afford the house by the end of the process, but within a few years, I get a text message that they just closed and need movers. During divorce, you need to be clear, patient, and persistent.

"Your life does not get better by chance, it gets better by change."

—JIM ROHN

CHAPTER 7

Oh Baby, Protect Those Babies

Here's a brutal truth: The person you are divorcing is someone that you chose to be your co-parent. You chose to have one, or sometimes more than one, child with this person. You knew who he/she was, you ignored who he/she was, and you now have this child or children. That person was your choice, not your child's choice, your mother's choice, or your best friend's choice. It was your choice. Therefore, you alone need to learn to co-parent with this person. You also need to be honest with yourself. Are you punishing your spouse because they are a terrible spouse, but you know in your soul that they are a good parent?

There is endless information on the internet on children and divorce. This is one area where you need to stand guard at the gates of your mind and avoid paralysis by analysis. You will hear terms like custody evaluator, guardian ad litem, co-parenting, alienation, co-parenting counseling, parentification, loyalty bind, and trauma. I will do my best to explain in simple terms my experience in this area.

Despite the legalese that you will need to know, there are some practical psychology tools that you should utilize as your foundation.

WHERE DO YOU START?

Here are some keys to start with:

- Do not use your children to punish your ex.

- Do not expect your spouse to be someone they are not now when the divorce is final.

- Accept who they are, and so long as they are a safe parent, they can grow into the other things too.

- Do not expect miracles. If this person was a fantastic communicator and full of empathy, you would still be together. That is not the case, so accept the reality and start co-parenting. There is not a single court in the country that can make a father be a dad. There is no court order that can mandate decency or give your children the parent that they deserve. If you are seeking that, save your time, save your money, accept reality, and move on.

Are your children really unsafe, or is that something your mind is creating so that you can keep them with you?

Not once have I had a case where kids are involved and the primary concern is not the child. No exceptions. In every single case, my clients always want "what is best for the child." However, there is litigation, because both parents have a very different definition of what that looks like. Your divorce, even the best divorce, will be an adverse childhood event for your child. It is up to you whether you create one trauma that they need to survive or many. We will talk about the difference between unhappy and dangerous. Now, let's get to protecting those babies.

For most parents, the first thing they think when divorce is happening is, "What will happen to my children?" How will you be without your babies for even a day? What if they get hurt when they're not in your presence? If you are like every other person that has ever been through divorce, this is normal. I can tell you today that it will be okay. Your children can thrive with two healthy, happy parents after divorce, even though they will not be living in the same house. Studies show that children who are exposed to serious conflict in their parents' marriage are better off when conflict is reduced.[5] If you have anxiety in this situation, examine where that is coming from. Is it coming from your own helicopter mom or is it real? Is there real danger?

YOUR CHILDREN CAN THRIVE WITH TWO HEALTHY, HAPPY PARENTS AFTER DIVORCE, EVEN THOUGH THEY WILL NOT BE LIVING IN THE SAME HOUSE.

I can also promise you that the first Saturday that you are home alone in the house, you may feel a gamut of emotions. Maybe being alone feels like quiet magic because you haven't had a day to yourself since your kids were born. The house will be still, you will be able to eat, drink, and do whatever your heart desires. Or maybe it's horrible. Maybe you can't sit at home without your kids and everything you see or do reminds you of them. For many moms, it's both extremes.

Most mothers have never had a quiet house with nothing to do but make themselves happy. Your first hours alone may be magical, but then the quiet really sets in, the feeling of loneliness sets in, and by the night-time it is eerie. That first night alone in the quiet will be the strangest feeling, but this too will become normal. It might feel peaceful, it might feel sad, it might feel scary.

Regardless of your circumstance, use this time to feel the feels. The most important lesson here is to avoid making this lonely, quiet feeling the responsibility of your child. When they return, never say, "I missed you." Instead say, "I love you. I am glad you enjoyed your time away." Our children are not here to fill our voids. They deserve their own peace in this process.

5 Paul Amato & Alan Booth, A Generation at Risk 237 (1997) [hereinafter Amato & Booth, Generation]; Paul Amato, Good Enough Marriages: Parental Discord, Divorce and Children's Long-term Wellbeing, 9 Va. J. Soc. Pol'y. & L.

OUR CHILDREN ARE NOT HERE
TO FILL OUR VOIDS.

KIDS KNOW MORE THAN WE THINK THEY DO

The saddest thing that I had to deal with in my own relationship was the reality that things were going to change for my children, and that the change was going to be dramatic. I knew that the holidays together were over. I knew that every other year I would miss the magical Christmas morning that we had created together. The waking up on Christmas morning and "normal" for them was over. They had no idea that Christmas morning for me was a chore and task that had to be survived just for them when things were at their worst. I had to come to the realization that there were going to be holidays where I was going to be alone. The words "holiday" and "alone" were defeating, until I redefined that a holiday alone was going to be vacation time to explore. I knew what they did not: I knew that they were going to have to adjust to an entirely new normal.

What I didn't know and appreciate was that the picture-perfect show that we were putting on was not at all picture-perfect. They knew about the fights behind closed doors. They knew that at holiday parties, their parents were talking to everyone but each other. It doesn't take a psychological genius to know that they saw the discord, and maybe, just maybe, holidays were not peaceful for them, either. The message here is that you might be deceiving yourself. Your children may not be happy. They may be in need of a change too.

Client Story

Home Seclusion

It is always a surprise when I meet with a woman for the first time and we talk about the babies, and from the mouths of babes, there is truth. In one case, I represented a woman that had been in a secluded marriage for many years. She stayed in her bedroom whenever she was home because the chance of running into her spouse throughout the house was sure to cause a fight, which sometimes got violent. It was easier for her to just seclude herself in one room of the house instead of the alternative.

I met with this woman for a couple of months before she decided that it was time to leave. When I asked her what changed her mind, she said, "Last night, my son called me into his room to kiss him good-night. After I kissed him, he said, 'When are we leaving?' Shocked, I asked, 'What do you mean?' He said, 'When are we leaving this place so that we can both be safe?'"

This was a woman that was suffering in the marriage because she didn't want to disrupt her son's routine. She couldn't stand the thought of him having to adjust to the new normal and for that adjustment to come at the heels of her choice to leave the marriage. She also thought that she had suffered in silence and suffered in seclusion, away from the watchful eyes of babes. However, her little child knew the entire time that his family was not okay. He knew that his mom was not safe. He knew that, in turn, he was not safe.

If you need an accurate mirror as to what is going on in your house, look at your child. Your children will model your behavior, they will model your relationship. Their future relationship is the relationship that you and your spouse are modeling for them right now. If you don't like what you see in that mirror, you need to change it.

I have more stories than I care to share where children have choked the dog because they saw Dad choke Mom, or where children have been downright cruel to their siblings. Why? Because they have watched their parents be cruel to each other. Most children will not tell you how they feel, but they will show you. Their behaviors of kicking other kids at school, or wetting the bed when they are years past potty training, are telling. Their behaviors are the looking glass. When you think that you are doing your children a massive service by remaining in the relationship, know that they know the happiness ship has sailed away. You also need to know that they have seen, heard, and experienced more than you have shared. Like you, they are trying to find their way through this divorce. They are also looking for answers and peace.

Imagine what you want to see in the mirror of your children. Are your children happy? Kind? Successful? Are they in a relationship where their partner holds their hand, just because they want to be near them? Are they in a relationship where there is kindness, mutual respect, and deep, enduring love? If you want them to have it, you need to find it and model it for them. If you think that your child does not really know what is going on, you are wrong. This is not a license to share with them in adult terms what is happening. It is just a reflection on what they already know. Just like you, your children will need therapy, consistency, and support through this process.

YOU CAN FRAME THE DIVORCE EXPERIENCE FOR YOUR CHILDREN

Divorce will change things for your child. What is important is how you frame that change. If you frame it in a box of sadness, challenge, uncertainty, and despair, your children will put the dismantling of your marriage in the same box. If you frame it in a box of new beginnings, new opportunities, and a new adventure, they will have the same experience.

> DIVORCE WILL CHANGE THINGS FOR YOUR CHILD. WHAT IS IMPORTANT IS HOW YOU FRAME THAT CHANGE.

You get to decide whether this is the beginning or the end, and how you decide to frame this transition will have a lasting impact on your babies— not just what they experience right now during the acute trauma, but how they will experience this in the future. They will be sad like you, and they will go through their own emotions. The important part of this conversation is that you never put your sadness, challenge, uncertainty, and despair on them. It's too much for a little back to carry.

KEEP YOUR DESPAIR TO YOURSELF

I can tell you that the saddest thing that you can do to your children is share your despair. Never share your despair. Never. Whenever I am court-appointed to represent children as their guardian, those children whose trauma has the strongest hold on them are the ones who have parents who have shared too much in the spirit of transparency and honesty because they don't want to lie to their child. But let's get real: we all lie to our children. If you disagree, tell me about the Easter Bunny.

Failing to keep despair to yourself isn't always obvious, especially if you're grieving. You might do it without even knowing that you are doing it. For example, its bedtime and your little guy knows that you are sad, despite the strong face you put on to get him to bed. Then he asks, "Mom, what's wrong?" with sweet concern. It would be so easy to fold and share that you are sad over the divorce or sad over something that Dad did. It is so easy to off-load because you know this little being loves you unconditionally. That is the exact wrong thing to do; that is the way you take all your hurt and put it on the little guy. How do I know? Because I have been there at bedtime when honesty would have been so easy for me, and so bad for my little guy.

Your children are half of you and half of your spouse. If they only hear "your dad is a loser," "your dad abandoned us," "your dad is a lying cheater," or "your dad can't be trusted," what they hear is: "I am a loser." "I can't be trusted." "I am a liar."

In one case, the child was so aligned with her mother who was in the depths of depression over the divorce that this 10-year-old bright lovely child tried to convince me that she knew the routine. Even if her mom was too tired or drugged or hungover to get her to school in the morning, she knew the routine and could do it herself. This little child had taken on the role of protecting her mother, because her mother shared too much. Her mother made the child responsible for her own feelings. Just before this book went to publication, I got a call that this child died of a drug overdose.

Just like your children know that you are unhappy cohabitating, they know how you feel, without you ever saying a word. In leaving a relationship and designing that new normal, don't substitute your child for a qualified therapist. Do not replace the codependency that you had with your spouse with your child.

IN LEAVING A RELATIONSHIP AND DESIGNING THAT NEW NORMAL, DON'T SUBSTITUTE YOUR CHILD FOR A QUALIFIED THERAPIST.

I have seen many clients get this wrong. I have also seen many clients get this right. You are not doing your child any favors telling them who the other parent really is. This is not a service to them. If your spouse is truly a loser, your child will learn that in their own time. You do not need to share this information with them. If your child knows too much, you are not protecting them. In the words of my favorite client, "The high road is lonely." Take it anyway.

Getting this part right matters. There are some things that you should never do. Never share your feelings, communications about your co-parenting, court papers, or voicemails regarding the divorce with your child. If you are talking with someone about it and they are in the house, assume that they are listening. If you ask me how to protect your babies, I'll tell you this is the first step.

Client Story
Do It for the Kids

During one particularly bitter divorce that had gone on for three years and cost the couple hundreds of thousands of dollars, there were two loving and well-adjusted children sitting in the court hallway.

The parents, on the other hand, were a mess. When there were hearings, the judge would have her bailiff bring in the parents separately, because sitting together in the courtroom was sure to cause a brawl and an arrest.

These two were horrendous to each other, the kind of ugly that would make for an exceptionally dramatic television show. During one hearing, the wife actually testified that she never loved the spouse and that it was always a business arrangement, so why would the judge grant her any less of the business property? On the flip side was a man that thought he had found his queen and surely loved her before the dissolution started.

I asked my client, "How do you do it?" He said, "I am raising three little men, and they have to know how to treat a woman."

In private, he regularly referred to his ex as Satan, but in front of those children, both parents held it together.

This reminds me of another similar case, where again, the woman had just been horrible to the father. For example, she would protest when the child would hug her father at public events. She made her disdain for her ex absolutely apparent. On Father's Day, she would only allow Dad an hour of time, because it was otherwise "her day."

On the flip side, for Mother's Day, he took his daughter shopping to purchase her mother a nice gift. He had his daughter call her mother when there was good news to share. He made it a point to make that relationship special for his daughter. Again, when I asked, "How do you do it?" and "Why do you do it?" Why pay me tens of thousands of dollars to fight these issues in court, only to then take his child to shop for her mother? He said, "I am the most important man in my daughter's life. I will teach her what to expect from men and what she should accept. It is my responsibility to show her how a man should treat a woman. If I treat her mother the way that she treats me, my daughter will learn that it is okay for a man to mistreat a woman, and she will tolerate a man that mistreats her."

I have very few female clients that are able to reciprocate the importance of this mirroring behavior so gracefully.

Maybe now, after reading *Cry All You Want*, you will find the tools you need to make this shift for your children. You are the model for your children, so what are you modeling?

DO IT FOR THE KIDS

Regardless of what happens in court and how nasty things get, remember that your kids deserve to love both parents. They also deserve a relationship with both parents. Go back to the first paragraph in this chapter and remember that you chose this person. That relationship may not look like what you want it to look like and you may end up regularly doing the heavy lifting for parenting duties, but don't make the other parent the villain in any story. Blame the judge, blame the lawyers, blame the law. Never blame the other parent to the child, even if it is the truth. If we all had the parents that we wanted—or even deserved—we would not have the lives that we have. The parents we have are part of our overall evolution. Read *What Happened to You?* by Bruce D. Perry, MD, PhD, and Oprah Winfrey; they outline that very clearly in their writing.

NEVER BLAME THE OTHER PARENT TO THE CHILD, EVEN IF IT IS THE TRUTH.

I have had many clients say, "I am not going to lie to my child about who his father is." I am not advocating lying. I am advocating finding the necessary skills and tools to grieve your trauma without transferring that trauma to your children. If your spouse is the scum from the bottom of the pool after winter, your children will learn on their own; you don't have to be the messenger. Hey, Easter Bunny, remember that we all lie to our kids when it is beneficial for them. It's called parenting.

Remember that hurt people hurt people. If you do not have the necessary skills and tools to handle your own emotions, your hurt will transfer to your kids.

When my daughter was born, she was deathly sick. She was three months old and dying in the hospital. I had seen her deteriorate since birth. I prayed, night after night, for her survival. I prayed as all mothers would: *God, make me sick and make her better. Let me carry this for her so she does not have to.* There is not a mother that would not choose to take on the pain so that her child would not have to. Divorce is where you can prove it. You need to handle the hard pain and emotions so that your child does not have to. This is your chance to live that principle.

ACCEPT CHANGE AND RELY ON RESILIENCY

How do you live that principle? You accept that change happens. Have you ever planned a fun outing for your kids, but when you wake up in the morning, it's raining, and the zoo is simply a no-go? You sheepishly call the kids into the living room to break the news that the zoo is not happening because the rain just won't allow it. You explain that you were also really excited about the outing, but the rain just is not going to let up. To your absolute surprise, there are no meltdowns, and the kids say, "Can we watch Netflix?" and nonchalantly go back to what they were doing before. The simple fact of the matter is: Kids adapt. Your children are the most resilient creatures in your life. This departure from their normal will take adjustment, but they will make it through if you manage your own emotions and protect them.

> THE SIMPLE FACT OF THE MATTER IS: KIDS ADAPT. YOUR CHILDREN ARE THE MOST RESILIENT CREATURES IN YOUR LIFE.

When I told my husband that I was leaving, I was internally crushed to make the decision that my children and I would be moving from our large home to a 1,600-square-foot home. I had knots in my stomach about how they would take the fact that they could no longer use the living room corridor as a racetrack and that their new bedroom was too small for the bunk beds with slides that they had come to love. Instead of each having their own bathroom, all three kids would be sharing one bath. The yard of our previous home was big enough to literally have pony rides and a carnival for birthday parties, but that wouldn't happen anymore. In fact, our new living room wasn't big enough to host more than a couple of friends.

These things tormented me, yet to my amazement, they tormented only me. When we moved, my kids couldn't have cared less about these little things that were monumental to me. I learned firsthand that the story that I was telling myself about how much a big house mattered was totally irrelevant to my kids. They didn't care where we lived. They loved their birthday party at the ninja gym just as much as much as they loved the pony party. They couldn't have cared less that at Christmas the tree was 10 times smaller than they were used to and that the professional house decorator never arrived. Those things mattered to me but didn't matter to them.

> *Ask yourself: How are you punishing yourself over change that your kids do not care about? Think about whether the things that you are telling yourself will matter to your children. Make a list. Write down what you care about. Then ask yourself, "Is that true? Is that really true? How do I feel when I believe that is true? How do I feel when I believe the opposite?" Look at Byron Katie's* The Work *to take a deep dive here.*

I deceived myself in the same way when my kids had to move from private school to public school. Private school was something that mattered to me. It made no difference to them. They met new neighbors and made new friends. The agony that I put myself through was worthless and served no purpose. You need to take a close look and evaluate what it means to protect your children. You need to decide whether they need emotional protection or real physical protection.

DANGEROUS CO-PARENTS EXIST

Now that we have gone over what not to do, let's talk about how you protect those babies. First and foremost, they will survive. To date, I have read more books than I can count and there is no manual out there on how to raise a United States president. In short, cut yourself some slack as a parent. If there is one thing that I know to be true, it is that judges will protect your children if they are given the evidence to do so.

That being said, dangerous co-parents exist. When things were darkest in my marriage, my husband was not well. In fact, I was afraid of him, and the last thing that I was going to do was to leave my little children alone with him. You need to follow your instincts, and if your spouse is a danger to your children, you need to fight. As my dad has always told me, "Don't fight, but if you are forced to fight, you fight to win."

AS MY DAD HAS ALWAYS TOLD ME, "DON'T FIGHT, BUT IF YOU ARE FORCED TO FIGHT, YOU FIGHT TO WIN."

Know that there are no winners even when a dangerous co-parent is involved, because even if you win a victory in court, your children still have to adapt to the fact that they have an unhealthy parent.

Also, there is a fine line in deciding to fight a dangerous spouse. You can't be a drama queen during this process, but you also can't diminish a dangerous situation. You do not need to make it worse than it is, but it's important to see it for what it is. Therefore, in looking at that fine line, decide if you're being a drama queen and making the situation worse than it really is, or if your kids are really in danger.

Client Story
A Dangerous Situation

I had one client that knew in her soul that her spouse was dangerous. She had taught her children to duck in the car at a young age, because when she was being abused and would leave, her spouse would chase after her with a gun, sometimes shooting. When we started digging into her case, she explained the ducking and why her kids did it, all while telling me that he was a good father and would never hurt the children.

This fantasy continued on while we were in and out of court without success. She would complain bitterly about the situation, but I could never get enough specifics to remove the children from their father's care. We just didn't have enough evidence. I knew that she was afraid and afraid for her children, but I couldn't get her to a place to give me the ammunition that I needed. It finally took the oldest child going to school one day, walking into the principal's office, and telling her that she was not going home, ever. She sat there all day and explained the brutal abuse that she and the siblings were enduring. The principal had no choice but to call Child Protective Services.

In this case, it's not that Mom was bad or trying to protect Dad; it's that Mom was so abused that she had to tell herself stories that her spouse was fine—it was her survival mechanism. She was telling herself stories that her child was fine. The reality of her situation was too painful to look at, so she ignored it as a defense mechanism. More importantly, the thought of taking on this demon in court was terrifying. It was a battle; he was a terrible liar and a complete narcissist. It would be a tough charge to tell her story to the judge, because she was terrified to be in a room with this man. But she did it. She won.

You see, if you let your brain tell you that you are in danger, and your children are in danger, and you let your brain believe that you were abused, then it is a painful and dark place to come out of. If you tell yourself, "It will all be okay, it's not that bad," then your brain can protect itself because there is no danger to fight. Sugarcoating this client's situation had become a defense mechanism. Her children never had to return to their abusive father, and immediately after the truth came out, the entire family was able to heal. You see, you do not need to be a "victim" if this is happening in your family. Exchange the word "victim" for "survivor." The moral of the story is: Call a spade a spade. Don't make it worse than it is, but be honest. You need to be honest and give your lawyer the information that they need to protect your child. You need to work in therapy to get the courage that you need to take on the dangerous parent in court. This is the hardest battle that you will have in your entire life, but it is necessary if your children are really in danger.

If this is the case, ask the court for a guardian ad litem, which is an attorney for the kids. Ask the court for a psychological custody evaluator, which is someone that will do psychological tests of the entire family with a specialty in custody and trauma. This person will then make recommendations to the judge on what your kids need to be successful. If you are not in a position to afford these services, read the book by Dr. Bruce Perry and Oprah Winfrey, *What Happened to You?*, and implement the lessons.

Drama Doesn't Work for Anyone

Reality is a fine line, because if you are over-dramatic, you risk losing credibility across the board. I had another case where the mother first claimed that she was physically abused by the father (my client), which started six months after their separation. The judge then ordered supervised exchanges. The mother filed six separate domestic violence orders of protection, all of which were dismissed and never granted. She claimed telephone stalking during one of those domestic violence cases, which led to criminal charges. In New Mexico, criminal charges are automatic if a person has a temporary restraining order. Lo and behold, the criminal case was also dismissed.

The woman claimed that Dad was abusing the children and dangerous. She would tell this to anyone that would listen. All the while, during those supervised exchanges, she was caught on video accusing Dad of various things in front of the children. She claimed in court that Dad was not the dad, requiring a paternity test. She demanded supervised visits. She fought in court that Dad was a domestic violence abuser; it was proven that he was not. She even went as far as to put her daughter through a sexual abuse exam only for it to be unfounded.

This woman's allegations were so pervasive that the state's physicians that investigate child abuse, our Child Abuse Response Team, filed a notice with the court that they would not examine the children any further based on allegations of Mom, and they would only investigate if they had a court order from the judge.

This went on for years.

In the end, the judge found that the mother's allegations amounted to child abuse and the kids were removed from her care. Dad was granted sole legal custody and Mom has very limited visitation, all supervised. It will take the judge on the case retiring or dying for her to ever get her children back.

If my clients head down a road of drama without proof that what they're claiming is true, they do not stay my clients for long. If you know that what you are saying is a fabrication, or more dramatic than the truth, stop now, get help for yourself, and deal with those demons. Do not use the custody case to find significance, sympathy, or vengeance.

All of this is boiled down to one principle: Manage your emotions so that your children do not have to, tell the truth, know that the court process does work, and know that the greatest thing that you can do to protect your children is stop sharing any information about the divorce. Be very careful on how you carry yourself in front of them. If there was ever a time to get therapy, it is now. If you need Time Line Therapy®, then now is the time to get it. You need to do whatever it takes to resolve your anger, sadness, guilt, fear, and shame that led to this case. If you resolve those, you may come to one of two conclusions:

1. Your co-parent is not the devil and you need to work together, or

2. Your co-parent is absolutely dangerous and you now have the tools to take them on to tell your story.

Either way, your children will be protected.

"Connectedness has the power to counterbalance adversity."

—DR. BRUCE PERRY

CHAPTER 8

Learn How to Co-Parent

Let me start with this: your judge will protect your kids if given the evidence that your kids need protection. All the rest is co-parenting. Now, in past chapters I've given some examples that represent the extreme sides of the co-parenting coin. You could even call some of them co-parenting nightmares. However, most scenarios exist in the gray middle—one parent doesn't do homework with the kids or neglects to dress the children in weather-appropriate clothing. This middle area includes non-dangerous situations, although they can be neglectful. They include situations where the choices made by the other parent would not have been your choices, but they are not overall harmful. Most of these situations require learning how to co-parent as an adult looking out for the best interests of your children, not as a person trying to "get" your ex at every turn.

In my experience, judges will order some parenting classes when homework is missed or a sweatshirt is forgotten, but they won't remove the children from the other parent. You need to be very realistic in your goals, especially when you expect that some minor oversights will end in your ex no longer seeing the children. If homework isn't completed twice, bring it up, but don't use that as your basis for sole custody.

YOU NEED TO BE VERY REALISTIC IN YOUR GOALS ESPECIALLY WHEN YOU EXPECT THAT SOME MINOR OVERSIGHTS WILL END IN YOUR EX NO LONGER SEEING THE CHILDREN.

The gray area offers an opportunity to do that awful and dreaded word: "co-parent." This is where all of your skills will be utilized to get the best outcome for your children. Because the small stuff does matter—homework matters, healthy meals matter, completing school projects on time matters. This is where learning to communicate your children's needs to the other parent will be paramount, and most importantly, communicating those needs without blame will get you the best success.

WATCH FOR PARENTIFICATION

Now, there are some things that don't look apparently dangerous to your child's well-being that are in fact the worst. The first is the word parentified, or parentification.

Parentification starts when the parent uses the child as a confidant, as moral support, as a friend. In these cases, the children feel a heavy burden placed on them, a burden that they don't know how to handle or what to do with. The children are often scared after listening to things that are well beyond their ability to understand and totally inappropriate for them to hear. If there is anything that you do, please don't talk about this divorce or the other parent in front of the children or within their earshot. Do not make your children responsible for your emotions. They cannot handle it and it is harmful to them.

Parentification is so sad, and it is so easy to do. It is a dangerous trap that even well-meaning parents fall into. After all, you're sad, you're upset, and you have this little child that just wants to hug your sadness away. It is so easy to share why you are sad. It is so easy to just tell them the "truth" about what is going on. However, that is not what is best for them, and your "truth" could permanently harm them. What if I told you that if you do this, your child is more likely to be an addict, more likely to suffer from depression and long-term mental effects? Would you stop? Please read on.

Parentification can cause depressive symptoms and anxiety, among other behavioral issues and disorders, including impeding interpersonal relationships, even with the person's own children.[6]

- These children are more susceptible to depression and anxiety.

- They may have more somatic symptoms such as headaches and stomachaches.

- They are more likely to be aggressive and disruptive, abuse substances, cause self-harm, and suffer from attention-deficit/ hyperactivity disorder.

- They also may struggle with interpersonal relationships.

I lived the parentification trap also.

If there was a lottery for all the crappy things to happen, I won it. However, I could not get to the good if I didn't go through the bad. I could not have served my clients in the way that I did if I had the life I wanted. My 18-year-old stepdaughter is the definition of a parentified child. Her mother made this little child, age 10, her emotional support beacon. She told this child everything that was good and bad in the world, but really focused on the bad. My stepdaughter became responsible for her mother's feelings. It was so out of control that the day my stepdaughter graduated from high school, her mom announced her engagement. She could not stand for anyone to have the attention but herself.

My stepdaughter moved out of her mother's home shortly after because handling her mother's divorce and bad choices and the need to compete with her for attention was overwhelming. This mother made her child responsible for her feelings. She created deep, lasting emotional scars. If you are doing this, now is the time to stop.

6 https://www.tc.columbia.edu/media/centers/gsjp/gsjp-volume-pdfs/25227_Engelhardt_Parentification.pdf

AVOID PARENTAL ALIENATION

In addition to parentification, there is something called parental alienation. Parental alienation happens when the child becomes estranged from one parent as a result of the psychological manipulation of the other parent. The child's estrangement manifests as fear, disrespect, or hostility toward the other parent.

If you choose to alienate, or the other parent engages in this behavior, it will be the most toxic and expensive battle that you will have with your ex. It will also be a sure way to destroy your child. Your little baby is not a soldier in your army to defeat your ex; they are a little life that deserves the chance to avoid trauma.

HOW DOES PARENTAL ALIENATION HAPPEN?

1. You or your co-parent tells your children details about the divorce. Adult details are not appropriate to share with the children. It is not always helpful to tell children your truth. I am not suggesting that you lie. I am saying if the other parent is a true asshole, your kids will learn about that in their own time and in their own way. You do not need to help them out here.

2. Some parents use this as a weapon to damage the other person's reputation or to simply punish them through the courts. This is not a place where you go to resolve your own childhood. Unresolved prior trauma should not be projected into this situation. In almost every case where sexual abuse has been alleged, the parent alleging the abuse was also abused as a child. Take these examinations closely.

3. You or your spouse speaks badly about the other parent in front of the children. This is where you openly blame the other spouse for all that is wrong in your life, in front of your kids. We can't go on vacation because your dad didn't consent to the trip. You can't play soccer because Dad won't pay half. This is the game.

4. You or your spouse uses negative body language when talking about the other parent. This is the rolling of eyes when you are in the same room or being physically hostile when you talk about them. You may be saying nothing, but your kids see and feel this. Knock it off.

5. Your children feel guilty when spending time with you, which is known as a loyalty bind. This is where you make the kids feel bad about going to the other parent, saying things like, "I really miss you when you are gone," "I wish you didn't have to go," or "Wouldn't you like to be here more?" All of these things cause loyalty binds. I also lived this one. Every time that I offered to take my stepdaughter shopping, her mother would say— sarcastically—"How nice." After the parentification started, the response was always "No, my mom will buy me that," when in fact that was never the case and would never happen.

6. Your children are interrogated by you or your ex. This happens when, every time that they come back from your ex, you use them for information. Where did you go? Who did you see? What did you eat? Who slept over? Who drove? All of those harmless-sounding questions are just the opposite. Do not interrogate your kids when they get home. Remind yourself that their other parent was your choice. Also know that if your children are in danger and experiencing bad events, they will tell you or a therapist. More importantly, as we discussed in the prior chapter, they will show you through behaviors. If you keep asking the questions, they will give you the answers that they think you want to hear. Be careful. If you need the child to "tell their story," only allow it in the context of therapy.

7. You withhold the children. You need to accept that your children have a God-given right to be happy. They have a right to thrive through this divorce and your decisions. If the other parent wants to take them on a trip, let them go. If Grandma wants to pick them up one afternoon a week, let it happen. You

need to not use your children to control any part of this process or any part of your emotions. Give them a chance to be happy. If the request from the other side is not going to hurt your kids, really consider if you need to deny it.

8. You give your children choices about the visits. This means that you don't make them go, or make it seem that this is their idea. One, they cannot handle that kind of pressure. This is not their decision; it is yours. Now you tell them, "Your father and I decided that (fill in the blank) is going to be the schedule." It is the adult's choice. They will start telling you that they don't want to go to make you feel better. They will tell Dad that they don't want to come with you to make him feel better. This is where your kids start being chameleon children. They are someone different in each house.

9. You ask your children what they want. This seems so simple, so realistic. It's not. Never, ever ask your kids what they want. What they want is for you and Dad to get back together, to move back into the big house, to eat dinner together every night, and to have both parents happy, loving, and peaceful in the same home. That is not reality, just like asking them what they want is not reality. You can't give them what they want. Even if they actually tell you the truth

10. You tell your children when you are going to court and share court pleadings, communication with the other parent, or communication between the lawyers. Anytime you share this, it is harmful. I have one case that takes up 19 banker's boxes. When the child reaches adulthood, if she wants to know what happened to her, it's all there. As a child, there is zero reason for her to access it now.

Rest assured, if you are engaging in any of these activities, you are doing yourself and your children no favors. If your spouse is doing this stuff, it must stop. At point, the judge is going to hear the truth and see what is happening, and it is certain that it will not end well for the parent doing this stuff. Your kids deserve to be happy, with their own definition of happy. If your spouse is doing it, get your children in therapy at all costs. The judge may need to order it, but your kids need a professional advocate to process these behaviors. This is one of those times that you need to fight to win.

CHECKING IN WITH LOYALTY BINDS

Loyalty binds are toxic and will destroy those babies of yours. These binds have you make it known, consciously or unconsciously, that you do not want your child to enjoy their time with the other parent. This is where you promise things that you cannot deliver for the sole purpose of being the "winning" and "favorite" parent.

A loyalty bind causes you to make your child choose between parents. For example, with my stepdaughter, every time that I offered to buy her clothes, send her to private school, or otherwise help her, her mother created a loyalty bind. She would tell her, "You don't need clothes; we will go shopping next weekend."

My stepdaughter's mother would always decline our offers to take care of her. Guess what? The things that she promised to keep my stepdaughter away from us never came. But it wasn't about the clothes to the mother, it was about the bind. It was about winning the affection, even when she couldn't deliver. How do you stop a loyalty bind? Let your child take things and clothing back and forth; let them enjoy the other parent and other family. Remember that this co-parent was your choice.

EFFECTIVE BLAME CAN BE USEFUL

If you are going to blame someone for all of the bad in your life, blame them effectively and blame them for all the good too. They might be a terrible co-parent, but without them, your child would not exist.

In our office, we utilize a tool called perceptual positioning. It is a neural-language processing (NLP) technique that might give you your first tool in this situation. Here is how it works: You get three pieces of paper and write the numbers 1, 2, and 3. You might ask an NLP practitioner to walk you through the process. This is where it gets hokey. You ask yourself, "Is it okay for my unconscious mind to resolve the conflict that I have with this person and do so consciously?"

In our scenario, the person that we are talking about is your co-parent. You put the number one on the floor facing the number two. Put the papers about three feet apart so that you can pretend that the number two is your co-parent. Then you put the number three in the middle and to the side, as if it were a neutral observer. If you start this exercise, you cannot stop until it is complete. You cannot stop halfway.

Keep in mind that the intent of it is to put yourself in the other person's shoes. You say what you need to say and then you let the fictitious person in front of you respond. You'd be shocked by how many conflicts can be solved this way.

Step One: You physically stand on the number 1 and you tell the other parent everything that you are feeling. You let loose. The key is that you have to do so without blaming. For example, you can't say, "You don't care about the kids' education and are a failure at getting them to do their homework." Instead, say something like, "The kids' homework is important and I don't understand how you can't have them finish it." You stay in position 1 until you have said everything that you need to say. This means everything. Unburden your soul to tell them everything that you want them to know.

Step Two: You physically walk into the position of your co-parent and look back at yourself. You tell yourself what you think your co-parent would say. For example, "I don't get off work until 6 p.m. and that is the earliest that you will allow me to drop off the kids. I can't work less because then I would have less money to support everyone. Most nights, I have to choose between a hot meal, homework, and hygiene, knowing that if I make the wrong choice, you will be on me." You stay in position number 2 until everything that your partner has to say has been said to you. This is mindreading at its best. Trust me and keep going.

Step Three: You physically walk into position number 3. This is where the neutral observer of this conversation stands. Being as honest as possible, you tell yourself, in position 1 and in the other parent's position,

position 2, what you observed. You might come to the conclusion that your co-parent is doing the best that they can with the resources that they have available to them.

This is an excellent technique to have the fight with yourself before you have it with the other person. At a minimum, you will get the tools to tell the other parent what you need and what your children need without casting blame. I have had clients entirely solve their problems, with very limited conflict, using this technique. It's simple: If you are going to look for what is wrong, you will find it. If you are going to look for what is right, you will find it. In this example, you might be able to start the conversation with "I know that you get off work at six and by the time you get home with the kids, have dinner, and get them ready for bed at eight, there is limited time to complete homework. Is there something that I can do to assist to make sure this gets done? I can either make sure that the kids eat before they go, or perhaps we can agree to move bedtime to 8:30 so that it can all get in."

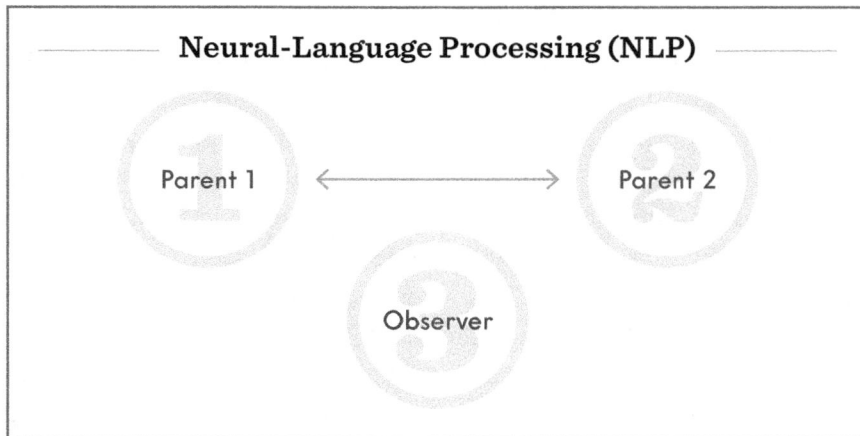

Neural-Language Processing (NLP)

Parent 1 ⟵⟶ Parent 2

Observer

IT'S SIMPLE: IF YOU ARE GOING TO LOOK FOR WHAT IS WRONG, YOU WILL FIND IT. IF YOU ARE GOING TO LOOK FOR WHAT IS RIGHT, YOU WILL FIND IT.

Now, this scenario works even when the other parent is not too busy, but is just entirely neglectful. For example, the other parent plays video games all night so homework is just not a priority. Again, if it is a fight that you cannot win, then do the homework before the kids leave, work with the teachers on what needs to be done so that the children do not fall behind, and document everything. Get yourself a calendar—not an app, but a handwritten calendar—where you can start to log all of the instances where homework is not done. See if there is a checklist that the teacher is willing to send home so that *both parents* can see what homework is due. Then you need to tell the other parent that you have an issue before you can get back to court.

Here is how that works: "I talked to Sammy's teacher and he told me that the reading log has not been done. It's in his red folder that is kept in his backpack. We each need to initial it every night after he reads for fifteen minutes." What you really want to say is, "I realize you don't give a shit about homework and can't read yourself, but can you please initial Sammy's homework so that he is not a failure like you?"

Which one gets you the better result?

Sadly, I have seen the latter more often. Then a week later, when the homework is still not done, you send another email message (text is awful for this purpose). "I sent you a message on Friday after talking to Sammy's teacher. I am not sure if you got it, but we each need to complete the reading log." What do you do in the interim? Sorry, but you make sure the reading log is done. You step up and spend your time reading. Then, after you have the proof that your co-parent is not going to step up, you do something about it. You can then walk into court with your 10 to 15 instances of when you politely and in a businesslike tone requested what you needed and what your children needed, and the other parent ignored it or otherwise did not do what was best for the children. Now you have proof and something that can get you a result.

I tell parents that the court process on these sorts of issues will do one of two things: It will teach your ex to step up and be the safe, caring parent that your children need, or it won't, and you will end up raising your children solo. Either way, your kids will win and get what they really need. The focus needs to be on the kids getting a win, not you proving a point.

> ## THE FOCUS NEEDS TO BE ON THE KIDS GETTING A WIN, NOT YOU PROVING A POINT.

I get it, your ex is a real asshat, but you can use parallel parenting to "co-parent" while the dust settles. This is a plan to have little or no interaction with your ex while you both enjoy the kids. It is not what is best, but it is better than one parent being removed. This also takes a great deal of trust that your child will be okay in the other home.

TREAT COMMUNICATION LIKE A BUSINESS

You are a smart woman. If you wouldn't send an email to your coworker like what you are sending to your ex, don't send it at all. If you would be embarrassed for your boss or new fling to read it, then don't send it. You need to keep all communication professional. Know that everything that you write, email, post on social media, or put on the internet is going to be seen by a judge. More importantly, many clients bring their parents and best friends in for moral support. Imagine their surprise when they listen in the courtroom to your foul behavior and words when you have cried to them for months about the viciousness of your ex. You will be judged on your words, so choose your words wisely.

I have a little daughter that is the most stubborn and persistent person alive. If I am frustrated with her and raise my voice and say, "Get your coat on," there is no chance that she is going to put her coat on. None. I might as well have changed our plans because we are not leaving the house anytime soon. However, if I smile and say, "It's time to leave; let's get our coats. Please, are you ready to take a ride in the car?" she can't put on her coat fast enough. Even if I am frustrated, if I pretend that I am not, she will respond with what I am requesting and needing from her. The same principle applies to your ex. You have an outcome that you need in this co-parenting relationship. Define that outcome and use your big-girl words to get what you need. If you have to fake it until you make it, do it.

In defining that outcome, don't expect a perfect parent standard from your spouse or yourself. The difficulty in parenting, especially parenting through a court battle, is that your actions are always judged in hindsight, where the judge has 20/20 vision, which was not afforded to you when you made the decision. If you expect perfection, you will end up broke and disappointed. If you expect that your children will be loved and cared for in a safe environment, you have a much better shot at a peaceful life. There have been instances where my children have had toaster waffles, that they prepared themselves, for dinner. There have been instances where bath time just didn't happen and the reading log was not going to get done. I have been the parent, more than once, where if my decisions and actions were being judged by a judge, it would not go well for me. However, my children have always been loved and are safe. Ask yourself if your standard is perfection for yourself or your co-parent, and if so, time to change the standard.

LETTING GO OF PERFECTION

Set a standard of what your children actually need, not what you want in a perfect world. You also have to realize that there will be times when you are running late to school and the wheels simply fall off. If you are understanding, your ex should reciprocate. They might not, but grace for yourself and grace for your co-parent can go a long way. Again, it can be lonely on the high road.

You may have thought that the most complicated relationship was the one that you have just left, but that is not true. The most complicated relationship that you will have will be this new relationship with your co-parent. You are now forced to raise a child with someone that you may not trust, may not like, and just decided to leave. This is not going to be an easy mental shift. In fact, it is going to be a massive mental twist. However, how you choose to adapt in this new relationship will be a deciding factor in how your children are raised.

THE MOST COMPLICATED RELATIONSHIP THAT YOU WILL HAVE WILL BE THIS NEW RELATIONSHIP WITH YOUR CO-PARENT.

The upside of what might be difficult co-parenting is that in the history of all my court cases, I have only had one case ever where, in my soul, I knew that the judge got it wrong. Therefore, in 999-plus cases, the judge got it right—or nearly right—and protected those babies. It might have taken time, money, and perseverance, but with the evidence, they got it right. The judges have a legal obligation to adhere to the "best interests of the children" standard. That means that if the evidence shows safety, then your child will be okay.

You need to accept your ex's faults, if they do not harm your child. The judge will accept your faults, if they do not harm the child. In my experience, judges generally start with the presumption that both parents love the children and both parents will make decisions that are best for the children. That means the new girlfriend might be obnoxious, but the judge will start with the idea that one parent will not choose someone harmful to the kids.

A CHILD-CENTERED DIVORCE

Is it possible that you chose a fantastic father or mother for your child, but this person is just not the spark that lights your bonfire heart? It is possible that this love for your child and the admiration of your spouse as a wonderful parent has led you to stay in the marriage longer than you would have if they were not such an admirable parent. If you answer yes to these questions, congratulations—you are about to learn how to protect those babies while helping them have a fulfilling relationship with both of you.

I understand that even if you are answering yes, it is still a heartache to not see your babies every day. I have represented a number of military men and women. One told me that he never left his wife because he couldn't imagine a day without his kids. Another knew that he was in a bad marriage and knew that his wife was not his soulmate. However, when the military deployed him to a war zone, he could not say "no" to his duty because he didn't want to leave his children. His duty called and he left without question for over a year. This is an extreme example, but it is clear that Americans do it all the time when duty calls and they are away from their children for months and years. Yet they are still bonded with their children and still engaged without daily physical contact. Once you let that soak in, we can talk about how you can move forward toward a child-centered divorce.

THE CO-PARENTING MIND TWIST

Sticks and stones may break my bones, but words will never hurt me.

As a linguist and someone who makes my money with my words, I can tell you that the phrase "sticks and stones may break my bones, but words will never hurt me" is simply not true. Words can give a worse lashing and create lasting pain.

Have you ever fallen down and not actually been physically injured, but you started crying? You were crying not because you were hurt, but because the thoughts and words in your brain have caused injury. The words that run through our minds in that moment create the tears. "Did everyone see that? They'll think I'm so clumsy. What if they laugh?" These thoughts and feelings of embarrassment can be crushing.

The language you use when communicating create your entire reality. Nothing has meaning until you assign a word to it. Words are how we evaluate our experiences. Words are how we create boxes in our life to think within. What do you need to know to determine that something is a toilet? You need words to define it. The problems that you are creating in your life have everything to do with the content of the communication.

This is no different when co-parenting. If you say that your children's father is an awful human, that is real. If you say that he is a flawed human, but a good parent, that is also real. You can find what is wrong with every situation, or you can find what is right.

I want to drive home the point that the words you use in co-parenting become the house you live in. The content of your communication—your words—are creating your entire life and entire world. The content of that communication will make the difference in your co-parenting relationship.

This means that you have to change the language, change the meaning, and take a different approach to co-parenting communication. It also means that you may be part of the problem. So when you stop being half of terrible co-parenting, you can get to a better solution. The problem that you are experiencing with the other parent is nothing more than a box that you have created with words that you now get to live in. Most often, I see that clients have put themselves in a box—usually it is the victim box, with language like "This always happens to me." "Why can't my co-parent understand?" "How can I trust this person?"

BE A SURVIVOR, NOT A VICTIM

Inductive language, empowered language, never comes from the place of a victim. It comes from the place of the survivor. When you approach your co-parenting communication from the place of the survivor, you can see things differently and apply a different approach. This is not a license for you to chant, "I am okay; nothing is wrong" all day. This is also not a license to mask the reality. This is a lesson on how to communicate from a different perspective.

How do you get there? I will use an example that I often see when the noncustodial parent wants to take the kids on a vacation outside of their parenting time and for a longer period than they have ever had alone. This is simple—and shouldn't be emotionally charged.

The victim approach will say that your partner is doing this to control you, to exert dominance, and to provide the kids with something that you cannot. The survivor approach asks these questions before responding:

- What would make this okay for me to say yes to?
- What is the harm in this situation?
- Is there really harm or is that a fallacy that I am creating all on my own?
- What is the benefit to my child if I agree to this?

- What goodwill might this create in my co-parenting relationship?

- How can I honor this request for my child to have the best experience while accepting my boundaries in this area?

- Do my boundaries serve me or my child?

As you start to ask yourself different questions in your co-parenting relationship, you start to create a different experience. Your nervous system—your brain—creates your entire life experience through your five senses: sight, hearing, touch, smell, and taste. All of these inputs into your nervous system are coded, ordered, and given meaning. The "given meaning" part is the important part of this conversation. The meaning that you assign to the communication may not be the intended meaning of the communication. Your brain takes in the communication and turns it into pictures, sounds, feelings, tastes, and words (self-talk). This is what you tell yourself about the communication that is coming your way. That means if the self-talk is always the victim protecting herself from the controlling co-parent, then you assign certain meaning to that.

As you take in information during an interaction, your brain runs an internal program. Now, this program has nothing to do with reality, but it creates your own personal reality. Your ability to examine your communication—and to discover and utilize the internal programs that you are running surrounding your ex by examining the communication between you—will help you achieve your desired co-parenting relationship. Even if your co-parent does not give a smidge to begin with, eventually the tide starts to turn, and communication gets better. If it does not, then you can go to a judge, explain your earnest effort at effective co-parenting, and seek intervention.

CONNECT WITH EMPATHY

Like a computer, you are running a program over and over. That could be: "My ex is a terrible person, father, and loser. He ruined my life." You run that program so consistently that you cannot see or feel anything different. You solve all problems from the corners of the box that say that your ex is a controlling loser and terrible father. You are deductive in your thinking.

The inverse is looking for the good. Looking for ways to get out of the program or box that you have put your ex into. Start by accepting that this person was your choice. Think back to why you made that choice. There were some good things, even if just for a moment, that led to this child. Think outwardly on the positive. There was at least one time that he made you laugh, smile, and feel special. If you have trouble with that, think of your ex as a child and imagine what that child must have been through to become what they are today. Find a way to have empathy. Then find a way to look for intent that is not negative.

At one time, my sister was in a terrible relationship. I asked my father why this person was brought into our lives. He said, without judgment, "Sometimes God puts these people in our lives because we are the only people that will pray for them." That is where I learned empathy, and I try to have my clients find the same empathy.

TAKE CARE WITH YOUR WORDS

If you can fix your communication, you can fix all that surrounds your communication. In more specific terms: If you focus on becoming a better co-parenting communicator, you will have a better life and your children will have a better life—even if the other side continues to communicate like a buffoon. If you want to find your stride with co-parenting, the way to begin is to assign positive intent to all communication, find empathy, and ask the inductive questions above. You can even put them on a sticky note near the computer where you write your responses so that you stay focused on what is possible.

IF YOU CAN FIX YOUR COMMUNICATION,
YOU CAN FIX ALL THAT SURROUNDS
YOUR COMMUNICATION.

There are some things that can help with this communication improvement, especially if you need some professional help to get out of the box.

- **The first thing** is to get a co-parenting coach. Even if your ex does not participate, this is to help you filter the communication and get coaching for your responses. This is someone to absorb the emotion so that the communication can be businesslike.

- **Second,** don't respond to communication immediately. When I get a nasty-gram from opposing counsel, my initial response is generally "eff off." That is not the right response, so I always leave those in my inbox for at least a day. Then I can respond without the initial emotion.

- **Third,** accept that all communication is coming from a place of good intent. You do not have to agree with the request, but it will change your experience if you allow your brain to assign the survivor language instead of the victim language.

- **Finally,** know that good communication is a model for your child. Also know that you left this relationship because communication was lacking somewhere, so don't look for a miracle, and accept imperfections—on both sides.

Think of it this way: Nothing exists in the world until you add words to define it. Therefore, in this situation, craft a definition that clearly serves your children. It is time that you learn to use your words and to use your language to achieve your specific and desired outcomes. The most eloquent way to describe this is in the words of Hafiz as delivered by Dr. Mario Garcia: "The words you declare become the house you live in." In this instance, the words you declare become the house that your children will live in. You need to decide whether it will be a free, happy, and safe place for them—or a prison. I am always saddened when parents cannot experience true joy with their children because they are waiting for them to reach age 18 so that they no longer have to deal with their ex or pay child support. That mentality robs you of the absolute magic of a small child in your life. Instead, know that your words can build or destroy that joy. This is within your control.

"THE WORDS YOU DECLARE BECOME THE HOUSE THAT YOUR CHILDREN WILL LIVE IN." YOU NEED TO DECIDE WHETHER IT WILL BE A FREE, HAPPY, AND SAFE PLACE FOR THEM—OR A PRISON.

LOOK FOR THE HIGHEST INTENT

If you assign meaning that is not intended to the language of your communication, you punish your ex for things that they did not create. Even worse, you punish yourself. In my life, it is fair to say that I am addicted to my work. The addiction has made my body exhausted and at times my emotions on a short wick. In the past, my husband would get upset if I had to work the weekend or was not home in time for dinner. In the past, I took his words and requests as nothing more than a way to control me and have me home to cook and be with the kids so he didn't have to do it. When I shifted my assignment of meaning to his words and actions, it shifted my entire experience of judgment surrounding the situation. Specifically, I began to tell myself, "His intent is for my greatest good. His intent is to have me home so that I can rest and enjoy our children and our wonderful life, not so that he can control me or control my addiction." How did I get there with the new assignment? I hired a coach, a fantastic coach who kept my values in line while refusing to allow me to tell stories to myself or others that simply were not true.

If you change how you assign communication from your ex, then you change the entire experience. Just try this, for a few weeks, without exception. Each time that you receive a communication from your ex, tell yourself, "He has [name of your child]'s best interest at heart. He wants what is best for her." By giving him grace in how you receive his communication, you are giving yourself compassion to stop the ongoing punishment. Now, there is always an exception (see the section on dangerous people and respond accordingly).

How do you resolve this intent issue in your, I know, "very different situation?" Guess what—in a thousand divorces, the themes are the same. Your exact situation might have different words assigned, but the themes are the same. If you take communication about your child's soccer tournament as everything but a soccer tournament, you assign meaning that this is your ex trying to control you, you assign meaning that this is his way to see you, this is his way to ruin your life—then that becomes your reality, in all communication, good or bad. Instead try, "This is just about soccer. Nothing more, nothing less, just about the weekend. His highest intent is for our son to play and enjoy the tournament." Turn what you are making ill intent into simple intent directed at the best interest of your child.

Please consider this: You can only effectively communicate if you are paying close attention to the "not only about" part of the question. The more "meaning" that you put into co-parenting communications, the more difficult it will be to silence the co-parenting saboteurs. You need to challenge the statements that are being made and always look for the higher intent. You both love your children—possibly very differently, because you learned the concept of "love" in different models of the world—so look for that highest intent, which will allow your children to actually be loved. In short, you both love your child differently, so you parent differently—accept that. Accept that the polarity between you is what caused this child to exist and find the silver lining in it.

> ## IN SHORT, YOU BOTH LOVE YOUR CHILD DIFFERENTLY, SO YOU PARENT DIFFERENTLY—ACCEPT THAT.

AIM FOR GOOD COMMUNICATION

The number one issue that I see after a divorce is finalized is poor co-parenting communication. It is fair to say that 98 percent of all co-parenting disputes after divorce could be solved with better co-parenting communication. The exceptions are one parent wanting to limit time-sharing unfairly (or with good cause) or one parenting wanting to relocate. All other disputes can be avoided with good communication.

The cornerstone to good communication is trust, and I know that you may not trust your ex right now, or ever again. You need to take whatever actions that you need to in order to release your own fears and anxiety so that you can rebuild the trust. Remember the earlier story about the lawyer that made the child out to be the slob? It is really easy to get tangled in that narrative and fight back. It is also really easy to ignore it. In this instance, ignore it and focus on the highest priority, which is to protect the child. This is the hardest thing that you will ever do. Your ex may have been emotionally or physically abusive to you, and now the court will likely require you to co-parent because your ex has never been a danger to the child.

Yes, I am telling you to communicate with someone when communication may have led to the breakdown of your relationship. As you are going through these hurt feelings and trying to navigate the new normal, I am sorry, but you need to make communication with your ex a cornerstone of your new co-parenting relationship.

YES, I AM TELLING YOU TO COMMUNICATE WITH SOMEONE WHEN COMMUNICATION MAY HAVE LED TO THE BREAKDOWN OF YOUR RELATIONSHIP.

It seems that in the era of instant communication, we can share our feelings, joys, and heartaches in under 140 characters on social media. Yet the idea of talking to your ex about your kids is painful. I suggest that you set that aside. Change that outlook right now. It is easy to communicate on social media or to send a scathing email because you do not have to see the reader's response. You do not have to feel the emotions that come along with it. This communication is no different. In short, you wouldn't arrive at a party and say half of the things you post in your memes online. The same holds true here. It is just easier to communicate in writing.

To help with better communication, look into website like Parenting Time or OurFamilyWizard, or apps that can bridge the communication gap so that you both remain focused on your kids. These tools take away the need to be present for the other's reaction. The following is an example of good communication and bad communication. You can decide which works better for you. If you can afford it, get a co-parenting coach.

This is what it looks like.

Spouse to You: *Jayce said that he wants to play soccer, and registration is starting. I will be taking him next week.*

Your Bad Response: *Why would I think that you are actually going to take him to soccer when you always sign him up for stuff and then leave it to me to figure out? This is not going to be one more thing that you disappoint him with. Did you forget that I am in college at night twice a week?*

Your Best Response: *Your question is: Can Jayce play soccer? My answer is no. At this time, I cannot commit the time and resources for soccer. If you have an alternate suggestion for his participation, please let me know.*

Poor Communication / You to Spouse: *Tommy wants to play soccer. I can't imagine that you would actually support him, so I will take care of it like everything else. Soccer practice is on Tuesdays, which is your night, so I will just keep him so I can take him to practice.*

Better Communication / You to Spouse: *Tommy wants to play soccer. The Little Kickers club has registration from the 1st to the 5th and the packet is attached. It costs $40 per week and we would need to split it. His age group practices on Tuesday night, which is your period of responsibility. If you cannot take him and agree, I will rearrange my schedule to drop him off. Will you agree for him to be enrolled in soccer?*

You want to give the other parent enough information to investigate a solution, and you need enough information to investigate a solution yourself. Don't just send off a pissed-off social media post attacking your ex. Every time that you send a tweet, Facebook message, text message, or email, imagine that the judge in your case will look at it someday. Imagine how embarrassed you will be when your communication is read out loud—by you—in a courtroom. A courtroom that your best friends and parents will be sitting in for moral support.

EVERY TIME THAT YOU SEND A TWEET, FACEBOOK MESSAGE, TEXT MESSAGE, OR EMAIL, IMAGINE THAT A JUDGE IN YOUR CASE WILL LOOK AT IT SOMEDAY.

Here are some pointers for better communication:

1. Give the other person enough information to actually investigate your request. Don't be afraid to Google your own information.

2. Give the other person time to respond. If your ex is a man, realize that men just need more time to process a request than women. Look into Alison Armstrong's work that talks about "waiting at the well." It means you ask a question, they will process it for days or sometimes weeks, but then they will come back with a certain answer.

3. Imagine the judge sitting on your shoulder while you write the email.

4. Imagine that your son or daughter will someday read that email. How will it make them feel about themselves? How will it make them feel about the conflict? How will it make them feel about your efforts to protect them from the conflict and not engage in it?

5. Ask a succinct question. If you cannot determine a succinct question in the moment, wait until you have boiled down

your request to one. If you are not sure that you really want something, wait until you are sure. It is the worst to say, "Can Sara play soccer?" then when your ex says yes, you say, "I changed my mind."

6. If you wouldn't send whatever message that you're sending to your boss, don't send it to your ex. If you wouldn't call your boss a controlling, lazy, and worthless sack, then don't call your ex that. To be fair, your boss might be controlling and lazy, but you would never say that out loud. Just because it is true, it does not mean that it should be shared.

7. Use a communication platform such as OurFamilyWizard that has a tone meter. It will tell you when you are being a jerk.

You always need to boil down all of the communication to "what is the question being asked?" and "what is my response to only the question being asked?" not "how do I feel about the question?" Don't process feelings and past hurts out loud and in script, but focus on what is needed for the child. Also, don't be a barrier to things that you don't really care about. If your parenting plan says that you have to give each other 30 days' notice for travel, and the grandparents just offered a visit to the Grand Canyon that is 20 days away, let the kids participate. This communication is not about you or controlling your ex with the kids or being controlled by the kids, but how you make sure that your kids have meaningful experiences.

I had one particular case where in every communication, my client called his ex-wife a whore. In fact, his ex-wife had chosen to exercise her rights in a free country and worked as an adult entertainer and companion for men on dates, but it was not helpful to the communication to attach the word "whore" to each message. It took a great deal of coaching, but the communication did improve when he decided to stop using antagonistic language.

Think of hiring a co-parenting counselor or coach. Don't consider the counseling to be something to repair the relationship, because most clients hear about "counseling" with their ex and they want no part of that party. However, co-parenting counseling focuses on setting aside the emotion while learning to communicate, not repairing the relationship. If you need help in this area and you just cannot set your own hurt aside, then you need to get help, because if you do not, you will spend a lot of money on things that the courts cannot change. It is okay to feel those emotions, it is okay to experience them, and you need to do so in a healthy and safe place. It is not okay to become those emotions.

IT IS OKAY TO FEEL THOSE EMOTIONS, IT IS OKAY TO EXPERIENCE THEM. IT IS NOT OKAY TO BECOME THOSE EMOTIONS.

Client Story

Fear and Anxiety

There was one client who allowed me to share her story because she became her fear and anxiety. When I met her, she owned a lovely spa in the poshest neighborhood. She was vibrant, successful, and self-made and she knew exactly what she wanted. You would never know that she was in a toxic marriage unless she told you. You could see the light beaming from this woman a mile away. She cared deeply about her clients, and her authentic, loving nature came through whether you walked in for a day of bliss or to buy a bottle of shampoo. Then there was that one day when she asked if I had a few minutes after my nail appointment, and of course I said sure.

I knew something was wrong because her light had dimmed. Her vibrant nature was absent. We sat down in a plush couples room and she told me the news. Her husband had asked for a divorce. She was beside herself. She knew that her marriage was toxic and not good for her, but she had three little boys that she adored, little boys that she could protect from her husband if she was with them every day. Little boys that would not have to learn who their father really was so long as she went home, played the part, and protected them from him.

He was the worst kind of violent, a master manipulator of all situations. It seemed that if you listened to his words long enough you would also fall under his trance and genuinely believe what he said, questioning your own sanity. His disease was narcissistic personality disorder. If you're unfamiliar, it is a mental condition in which people have an inflated sense of self-importance, and a deep need for excessive attention and admiration. I think we all have healthy traits of a narcissist. However, if you come in contact with someone that has the disorder, they have troubled relationships and a lack of empathy for others. My friend, and now my client, had lost her light because she bought his version of who she was. That led to the weakness of anxiety taking over her entire world.

I see this often, but it's not often that the change becomes permanent. We got her through the divorce, and she eventually had her little guys full-time. However, the victories in court were not true victories because she never reclaimed herself. Free rent, remember that? She gave her ex-spouse free rent in her brain for years, and maybe in perpetuity. Almost 13 years later, I ran into her at my favorite coffee shop. Her two oldest sons were grown and off to college. She was having coffee with the youngest, gearing up for a new school year. She was still beautiful, but her light was gone. When we sat to chat while I waited for my favorite mac milk latte, she dumped into the pattern of how terrible her ex-spouse was, is, and continues to be. This many years later, she was still living in fear of what he would do or say next to manipulate her. She was still making the daily decision to give him free rent. She allowed him to control her life years after the divorce by allowing him to control her thoughts. She had been in therapy since the divorce and was still carrying the shame of divorce with her.

In her defense, her spouse was not the spouse that she deserved in her life. He was not the man that she wanted and needed him to be. His brain would not allow him to be. If you ask a doctor, personality disorders are the most difficult to diagnose and treat, and the most difficult for others to be around. He was not the father that her sons deserved. His love for them was always conditional on them feeding his narcissism. He wanted them to achieve—not for their benefit, but for his own, because it reflected how "he looked." My friend and this man had never been back to court, yet, despite the divorce being years in the past, it was still up front and personal for her. Her light was lost based on false evidence that appeared real.

Now, if you need specific help on how to deal with a narcissist, you need to seek professional coaching or counseling on the matter. It will not be without a challenge, but just know that if you let the narcissist live in your thoughts rent free, you cannot devote that valuable real estate to something else. Most importantly, know that they do not define your brand and you cannot buy into their version of you. There are endless blogs on divorcing a narcissist and valuable books to read on just this subject, but for the sake of our conversation, just remember: No more free rent. The narcissist cannot and will not ever appreciate you or feel empathy for you. It is not existent in their chemistry, so understand that. Do not seek empathy from them and get back to being yourself before the narcissist made you an image of them.

You get to decide what this means. You get to decide how to raise your kids, and your decisions will shape their outcome. Most importantly, let the love for yourself and your children outweigh the hurt and possible hate that you have for your ex-spouse. Differentiate between the facts and the emotions, and if you are going to fight, fight to win.

You cannot let your own anxiety control the communication and co-parenting. You cannot diagnose your ex. Stand guard at the gates of your mind and communicate what you earnestly believe is best for your children. If you need professional help, seek it. Bottom line, don't make co-parenting about anything other than raising your kids.

"If you don't heal the wounds of the past, you bleed into the future."

—IYANLA VANZANT

CHAPTER 9
Life after Divorce

How do you start a relationship with someone that you don't know? First, you get to know them. You learn what their likes and dislikes are. You learn how they like their food and what textures in their home make them gleam. You learn to be incredibly interested in the things that may not interest you. You go out of your way to look hot—and when you look hot, you feel hot. You wear those kinky boots that you save for Halloween, but they are also third-date appropriate. Finally, you make sure that you are in the best shape possible to lure in this great lover. Nothing is more important but enjoying this person.

What if that person was you? What if you applied your "dating" standards to yourself? What if you treated yourself the way you treat someone that you love?

How long has it been since you dressed in beautiful clothes that you like with no agenda but to enjoy the clothing? It can be anything from a jersey that you love with sweatpants to that chenille cardigan that waits in the closet every year for the first crisp morning. When was the last time that you got yourself ready in the morning to impress no one other than yourself? When was the last time you had dinner out at a fabulous restaurant and enjoyed not having to share your dessert? How would it feel to not only find yourself, but to reinvent yourself? Again, "going back" to who you were before the marriage is not a worthy goal. However, "living up" to the new standards that you now have in your life is enticing.

HOW WOULD IT FEEL TO NOT ONLY FIND YOURSELF, BUT TO REINVENT YOURSELF?

What if I told you that the same old thoughts create the same old you? How would you live your life every day if you thought that you could create your life? How would you show up each day if you knew that your thoughts created your future? What new thoughts would you have to create a new future? What if new thoughts created a new you? How would it feel to shed the skin of this marriage and start fresh?

In this chapter, I invite you to invent this woman that you are going to be tomorrow. If you want that compelling future, keep reading. When you leave a relationship, you need to replace it with another one. Some women replace it with a relationship with alcohol or other vices. The most powerful women replace it with a relationship with themselves.

I learned this lesson at a young age. I was in the seventh grade and helping a local woman clean her house. She had been married three times before and was getting married again. Because I didn't understand appropriate things to ask an adult, I asked her what was different in the fourth marriage. She said, "I realized that I needed to love myself first before I could expect anyone else to love me. This time, I love myself, so he can too." Ladies, it's time to find your love . . . for yourself.

FIND A COMPELLING FUTURE

When was the last time that you sat down and put pen to paper to decide what you want? When was the last time that you did something just for yourself, just for fun, or just because? How can you create a future that you want if you don't know what you want?

Earlier, we noted the study done by the American Bar Association where women are sent to a car dealership to negotiate a car price for their best friend and were then sent back to negotiate a car price for themselves. The woman always gets a better price and terms when she is negotiating for someone else. The basis is simple: Women do more for others than we are willing to do for ourselves. It's time to change that philosophy and treat yourself first. I know what I am asking, especially when the clothing, dining out, and other budgets have all been cut in half. However, determining what you want and like does not need to cost a fortune. It could be as simple as lighting the candles that your ex hated but that you love. It could be a long bath on your first night alone.

A compelling future needs to start with a relationship with yourself. You also have to know where you are now and where you want to go. What does it feel like when you get there? Imagine this: You are invited into the home of a 90-year-old woman, and that woman is you. What does her home look like? How is she dressed? How does she feel? This woman wants to give you advice. What does she tell you and what conversations do you have? Is she timid, weak, and full of regret? Or is she a force to be reckoned with, full of life, with her thinner skin and gray hair, with her stories full of laughter, fun, and wisdom—because she lived? Not perfectly, but she lived. She lived life on her own terms.

Would this woman tell you that you should have sulked longer after your divorce? Would she tell you that you should have cried harder? Would she tell you that the walls that you built around your heart served you well all those years later? Does she tell you that she lived? Does she have stories of unabashed laughter, love, and sex? As you reinvent this compelling future, ask yourself: What will your 90-year-old self tell you about the decisions that you are making, or the decisions that you are refusing to make?

AS YOU REINVENT THIS COMPELLING FUTURE, ASK YOURSELF: WHAT WILL YOUR 90-YEAR-OLD SELF TELL YOU ABOUT THE DECISIONS THAT YOU ARE MAKING, OR THE DECISIONS THAT YOU ARE REFUSING TO MAKE?

In 2016, I was assigned to a handful of court cases to represent the elderly. I had to travel around the state meeting my clients. I was so bitter, traveling all day to meet with a client on a case that I would never get paid for. I would think in those moments, "God is teaching me a different lesson."

After driving three hours and getting lost at least once, on a road that I was sure was where all horror movies start, I arrived at a private senior group home. It looked like a poorly built doublewide trailer that had been covered in stucco. I was sure that I was in the wrong place, but my GPS was dead-on. I walked inside and there was a kitchen where a helper was making spaghetti and frozen garlic bread. The cook seemed to have the culinary skills of an 18-year-old college freshman with a hot plate. I continued to the table to meet with my client. He was in his late 70s and he didn't look frail, but I could see the sadness in his eyes. We talked about his life and I learned that he was a truck driver and worked odd jobs throughout his life. He could no longer manage his own money or healthcare, and he had a state-appointed guardian and conservator that had stolen money from him. I was there to check up on him and to tell the judge how he was doing since his current court-ordered guardian was on the run from the feds. As we talked, I learned the greatest lesson of my career.

He had been married before and had a few children that he had not seen in too many years to count. He couldn't remember all of the places that he had lived, but he had fond memories of his military days. I started to wrap up our meeting because it was almost time for him to have the dreadful spaghetti dinner. I asked him, "What do you want the judge to know about you?" He said, "Tell him that I am sorry." I couldn't understand, so I reminded him that he had nothing to be sorry about. His actions had nothing to do with the current circumstances in the case. He again said, "Tell him that I am sorry." At that moment, the judge should have been the sorry one, seeing the conditions of this clean but cold home. Then he said, "Tell the judge that I am sorry that I never did anything with my life." He said, "I worked where I could, but then I never did another good thing."

He had deep regret for not living the life that he had set out to live. It was clear that he wanted more as a younger man, didn't pursue it, and now felt that it was too late. I could see that he was sincere and deeply troubled by the facts of his current circumstance, and that he did not feel that his life lived up to his expectations. I sat longer with him and joined him in eating the dreadful spaghetti, taking the time to understand how to avoid this regret in my own life. We parted ways that evening after I learned all of his life story that he could remember. We appeared in court a few weeks later, and over the phone, he said the same thing to the judge. In all my cases, this case taught me the lesson of regret. These cases that felt like a thorn provided me some of the best lessons of my career. This is the most important thing in creating your compelling future: Avoid regret. At all cost, avoid regret. If the old woman would be troubled by the way you are living and feeling, then change it now.

> ## THIS IS THE MOST IMPORTANT THING IN CREATING YOUR COMPELLING FUTURE: AVOID REGRET. AT ALL COST, AVOID REGRET.

COME TO YOUR OWN RESCUE

The first time that I learned about coming to my own rescue, I was already in college. Now, I had been on my own for a few years, but I'd also always had a boyfriend that could do those "man chores." I went to visit my elderly aunt and we arranged to go to lunch. Before we headed out, she said that she needed to change the lightbulbs in the kitchen, which were behind the old-style 1970s recessed fixtures. I said, "Okay, who is coming to do that?" She laughed and said, "We don't have anyone to do it; we are going to change them ourselves!" I was amazed as this little old lady grabbed her tools and her ladder, and we took apart the fixture, changed the lights, and put it all back together—this time clean, of course.

In that moment, I realized that I did not need someone else for man chores. I could do them myself. My husband would absolutely disagree. The lesson was that I *can* do it myself, not that I am *going to* in the future. As the years pass, and I continue to visit my fiercely independent aunt, she continues to inspire me to live according to my own rules. How, specifically?

Because she's 80 years old, I often ask her to come stay with me so that I can take care of her. She told me that she liked falling asleep on the couch and no one could tell her otherwise. She always reminds me, "I do what I want, when I want. I wear what I want, I eat what I want, and I answer to no one." This is not advice to stay single forever, but advice that you can enjoy your own company, you can take care of yourself, and if needed, you can do your own "man chores."

CREATE NEW ANCHORS

You have probably never heard of the term "anchor" as it's used in this book. In short, there is a reason that we love balsam and fir candles during the holiday and why stores can have that certain scent in the air to make us buy things. The anchors in our brains can be strong. Just as there are positive anchors—that feeling that you get when you lounge in a bath with vanilla and cardamom oil—and there can also be negative anchors. If you are at this stage in the book, there are certainly some negative anchors that you need to reprogram.

CLIENT STORY

Heartbreak Anchors

I had one particularly special client who loved receiving flowers. Who doesn't love the call from the front desk letting you know that you have a special delivery? On this day, my client had been in a number of fights with her spouse and she was certainly contemplating divorce, but she was in a loyalty bind, because like all of us, she loved her spouse. She knew that things were bad, but she had not yet found the tools to voice her needs. To make it more complicated, she had also become a caregiver for her spouse's mother. She rationalized his behavior as stress over his mother's condition. However, in plain legal terms his behavior was domestic violence.

She arrived at the front desk after another fight and saw the dozen long-stem roses from her favorite florist. She had received flowers before, but never like these—straight from a magazine. The reception-ist coddled, "Someone loves you." My client took the beautiful bouquet back to her desk to open the card. The card was not just the usual two-inch rectangle that can fit six perfectly spaced words. It was an envelope. As she returned to her desk, the office lookie-loos gathered around to ogle. She smiled at the attention and opened the letter. It was not the pleasant apology that she had hoped for. Instead, it was divorce papers.

She had suffered in silence, so not a soul knew what she was living through. As her eyes welled up with tears, she saw the title: "Petition for Dissolution of Marriage." She put the envelope down, smiled at her coworkers, and excused herself to the restroom, where she proceeded to be sick. Not sick because the divorce was imminent, but sick over how he could embarrass her this one last time. She was accustomed to checking her bank balance before a dinner out with the girls, because when the waiter came with the tab, she would find that he had can-celed her check card. She had been embarrassed before, but this was a new level, even for evil. She gathered her things to leave work, but saved the note, because someday the judge would need to see just how callous her spouse could be. In that instance, a negative anchor was created—she never wanted to receive flowers at work again. Sure, in our rational mind we know that not all flowers are bad, but the anchor was formed.

What anchors have you created in your life? Have you decided that hol-idays suck or attending your child's school plays are miserable because your ex is going to be there with his gawking mother, or worse, his new sex toy?

Maybe you have told yourself and made yourself believe a number of sto-ries that just are not true, and you would be much happier if you left those anchors at the bottom of the ocean and far away from your new journey.

In my own marriage, I did not like holidays. Not only did I not like them, but I would actively try to avoid them, and I was sure to make myself as miserable as possible, before, during, and after the holiday. Not because the celebration was in itself terrible, but because at the time, my spouse and I could not stand each other, and sitting for Christmas was always just an Academy Award–winning performance of pleasantries.

Those bad holiday anchors were strong, just as my client's anchor of getting flowers was. It was not one bad holiday that led to the anchor for me, but many. It seemed that my husband's issues always started just after Halloween, which made Thanksgiving a chore. Then by Christmas, we were dedicated to surviving the holiday together only for the sake of our children. Then we had to decide how to get out of New Year's Eve. It wasn't until our last year together, before he got help, that I had to skip the holiday altogether.

My assistant scheduled me a trip to an all-inclusive resort in Mexico. I packed up the family and left on Christmas morning. There was no need to buy gifts, wear a sweater that I hated, or attend any gathering to answer "fine" when asked how things were. It was that trip to Mexico that broke the anchor. Yes, the resort had a large fake pine tree in the lobby that overlooked the ocean, and we had Japanese food for Christmas dinner after spending the day lounging and avoiding all contact with the outside world. It helped that the very next year, my husband got the help that he needed, and holidays started being joyous again.

It is time to examine your anchors and decide which anchors are serving you and which anchors need to go. In creating the life that you want in the future, you will have a much better shot at success if you don't start with the decisions of the past. If you need some help identifying those anchors, work with your therapist to delve deeper or find someone in your area that does work as an NLP practitioner. Then unchain the anchors and move forward. Warning: If you hang out with me too long, I will brainwash you into knowing that you can achieve anything.

WARNING: IF YOU HANG OUT WITH
ME TOO LONG, I WILL BRAINWASH
YOU INTO KNOWING THAT YOU
CAN ACHIEVE ANYTHING.

In short, the tools you need start with self-love. Self-love is not manicures and Starbucks. It is caring for yourself at the deepest level above all other things. When you wake up tomorrow morning, try this on for size, see if it fits: "Every day, in every way, I am getting better."

At the end of this chapter, I hope that you write down your answers to the questions and that you create a vision for your future. Something compelling that excites you. That vision needs to include finding love again, starting with love for yourself. It is time to find that new identity and go create the woman of your dreams. She is in there—let her out to conquer all that is in front of you. Also know that if you do what you always did, you will get what you have always got. Therefore, you need to do something different, and that starts with different thoughts about yourself and your circumstance. It also requires different thoughts about your future and what it means to be free of your marriage.

If you tell yourself you are worthy of the effort, then you are worthy. If you tell yourself you are not, that will also be true.

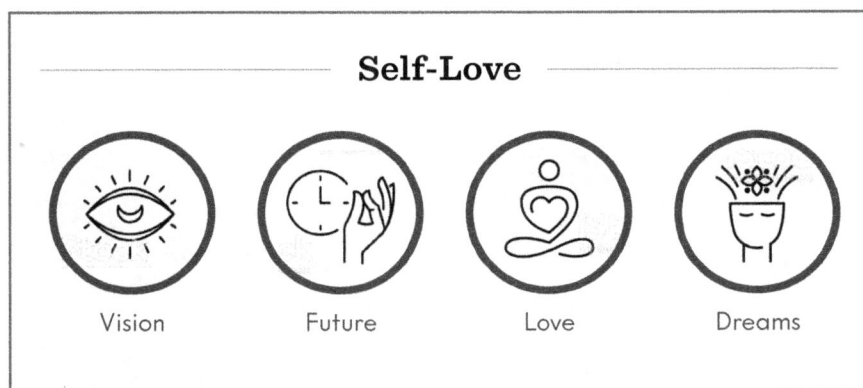

Self-Love

| Vision | Future | Love | Dreams |

A good incantation is "All of my needs and desires are being met beyond my expectations."

Cry All You Want. Just Get It Done.

Marriage is hard. Divorce is hard. Pick your hard and know that whatever you choose, you will survive. Your children will also survive.

I can't get inside of your head and make the "should you stay or should you go" decision for you. You have to decide that for yourself. What I can do, what my team can do, and what I hope *Cry All You Want* can do is give you the tools that you need to make the decision for yourself, and hopefully a community of support to let you feel the feels.

After participating in at least a thousand divorces—which I know sounds odd—I can tell you that the people who focus on what they want during the process win. These are the people who have the vision and strength to put emotions aside to create the best foundation for themselves and their children. These are the people who do not put their kids in the middle or start expensive, petty wars with their ex just to prove a point. You can do that. You can also do something very different.

But let's also be real. Getting to that point might take a bucket or swimming pool of tears. Not a problem. As my dad said, "Cry all you want. Just get it done!"

Pick up the pen that writes your story and get to work on your future. Make the choices that feel honest to you and congruent and in alignment with your goals. Follow your instincts. Make decisions that make you happy. For once in your life, do something—right now—just for you!

PICK UP THE PEN THAT WRITES YOUR STORY AND GET TO WORK ON YOUR FUTURE.

That activity, that focus on yourself, is the truly beautiful thing that can come from divorce (or the consideration of it). Throughout *Cry All You Want*, you've seen women and men who have come out better after making one of the toughest decisions in their lives. You can do the same. You can not only pick up the pieces but also arrange them in a way that lays a foundation for your best future.

Check out the resources, talk to the people you love who also love you back, take some time to figure out what you need to do to be whole again, and then get it done. Rely on professionals who can help you. Tell loved ones what you need. Protect yourself and paint your future.

I've walked down the road that you're going down. There's no two ways about it—the road is full of potholes and uncertainty. While your destination may be different from mine, you're guaranteed to have numerous crossovers in the journey. It's hard and it hurts, but it's up to you to decide for how long.

While *Cry All You Want* may be a starting point for you, if you are struggling to get to a point where you have some clarity in what you need from the end of the relationship, my team can help (if you live in New Mexico—if you don't, there are hundreds of professionals throughout the country who can do the same). The point is: You are not alone. You can do this. You can feel your emotions in safe places where they're not going to hurt your kids or your outcome. Day by day, month by month, you will heal.

YOU ARE NOT ALONE. YOU CAN DO THIS. DAY BY DAY, MONTH BY MONTH, YOU WILL HEAL.

I'm simply suggesting that you envision where you want to be when this cloud lifts. Where and how do you want to spend your healing days? What journey do you want to set for yourself when the sky turns to blue? Live today for the memories of your 90-year-old self in the future.

If I had the marriage that I wanted, then I would not be the lawyer that I am. My story has been a painful one, but as I look back at it, life did not happen *to* me; it happened *for* me.

Cry all you want. Just get it done.

You are not alone.

Sincerely,

Antonia Roybal-Mack

Worksheets

WORKSHEET #1

Remember, when evaluating these questions, ask yourself what advice you would give your best girlfriend or sister if she came to you with your story. If she came, and with brutal honesty, laid her marriage at your feet, would you tell her to get back in for another round or tap out? Again, the only rule here is: Be honest.

Take out your journal/paper and a pen, or your computer, and write down your answers to these questions.

Nothing is written in stone, merely ink, so answer with what you know and feel to be true in this very moment. Have courage—you are not alone!

1. Are the reasons you entered this marriage still valid today?

2. Are you happy? Do you know what happy looks like?

3. If nothing changes, can you see yourself in this marriage for the next six months? Year? Lifetime?

4. What needs to change so that you could see yourself in this marriage long term?

5. What things from question 4 are in your control?

6. What things from question 4 are in your spouse's control?

7. Are you willing to do anything, as long as it's legal, to change the things that you can change?

8. What are the things you desire in your life when you rise each morning? Do you just want peace? What does that look like?

9. What will your life look like in six months, a year, if you make no changes?

10. Can you accept the result?

11. Are you staying because you are too fearful or invested in the illusion of a happy marriage to accept reality?

You are doing great! Are you ready to go deeper? If so, here are some additional questions that might be relevant to your situation:

1. What is most important in your life?

2. What is the story you have been telling yourself? Is it true?

3. What do you believe about yourself?

4. What has your life been about until now?

5. What emotion is driving your life right now?

Now that you have more clarity and know what you are working with, keep going! You will only know the true answer if you ask yourself the right questions. Remember, there are no bad answers!

1. If you don't change this, what will it mean?

2. What will it cost you financially?

3. What will it cost you emotionally?

4. Who will it hurt if you don't make a change?

5. How has this been working for you?

Finally, the most important questions of all (none of which must be answered, by the way). Answering the previous questions before you complete this section is essential, for they prepare you to answer these:

1. What do you want versus what do you have?

2. What is preventing you from getting what you want?

3. Is what you want possible?

4. What is really stopping you from getting what you want?

5. What is really going on?

6. What does that mean?

7. What do you believe about separation or divorce?

WORKSHEET #2

The hardest part of my job, in any divorce consultation, is to tell my client that they should have left sooner.

- They should have left when they knew their spouse was cheating.
- They should have left five years ago when their spouse refused to work.
- They should have left after the first bad beating incident or the first time they called the police on their spouse.

Their decision to stay often led to very painful and damaging results. It didn't have to end that way if they had made other choices. If you are reading this, then you know it's time to decide. Ask yourself:

- How long do you want to stay?
- Have you stayed too long already?

These questions are coming from me, someone who, like many of my clients, has never given up on anything a day in my life. So, ask yourself:

- How many times have I felt that my spouse is dishonest with me?
- Why do I feel like my spouse is dishonest with me?
- What have I done about these feelings in the past?
- What is working with this person in my life, and what is not?
- How is my spouse adding to my joy and my life right now?
- What are the healthy lessons that my children are learning from this relationship?
- What are the unhealthy lessons that my children are learning from this relationship?
- If my daughter was going through the same thing, what would I tell her to do?

- What does happiness look like and how does that compare to the present facts?
- Am I staying in this relationship to prove that I am lovable?
- Is this relationship an attempt for me to gain self-love? If so, is this a good and healthy permanent way to get self-love?
- Can I do this for another day?
- Can I do this for another hour?
- Can I do this for another minute?
- What is stopping me?

BUSINESS BANK ACCOUNT WORKSHEET

BANK ACCOUNTS/CREDIT UNION ACCOUNTS

*Type of Account	Name & Address of Institution	Account #	Names on Account	Date Opened	Date Closed	Current Balance

*Savings or Checking

CREDIT UNION ACCOUNTS

*Type of Account	Name & Address of Institution	Account #	Names on Account	Date Opened	Date Closed	Current Balance

*Savings or Checking

CDs

Name & Address of Institution	Account #	Names on Account	Date Opened	Date Closed	Current Balance

TRUST ACCOUNTS

Name & Address of Institution	Account #	Names on Account	Date Opened	Date Closed	Current Balance

OTHER ACCOUNTS

*Type of Account	Name & Address of Institution	Account #	Names on Account	Date Opened	Date Closed	Current Balance

Include money markets, mutual funds, ready assets, cash management accounts, etc.

BUSINESS INTERESTS WORKSHEET

NAME OF BUSINESS: _____

PRESENT POSITION OR RELATIONSHIP: _____

INCOME

List the total gross of all INCOME you received from the business in each of the last three years:

YEAR	TOTAL RECEIVED

VALUE OF INTEREST

PRESENT VALUE OF BUSINESS	
NUMBER OF SHARES, PERCENTAGE INTEREST, OR OTHER MEASURE OF YOUR INTEREST IN THE BUSINESS	
DESCRIBE THE METHOD USED TO DETERMINE THE VALUE OF THE BUSINESS AND YOUR SHARE OF THAT VALUE	

HISTORY

DATE OF INITIAL INVOLVEMENT		
AMOUNT OF ANY ASSETS OR MONEY LENT OR TRANSFERRED TO BUSINESS	1) At start-up:	
	2) Since start-up (describe each separately):	
	3) IDENTIFY any DOCUMENT showing or tending to show in any way the information requested above.	

DEBTS

Do you owe the business money? YES ☐ NO ☐

If "yes":

☐ Amount presently owed:

☐ Original amount owed:

☐ Terms for repayment:

☐ Describe the nature of the debt and state the reason it was incurred:

Does the business owe you any money? YES ☐ NO ☐

☐ Amount presently owed:

☐ Original amount owed:

☐ Terms for payment:

Provide the date and amount of each payment made to you or on your behalf.

DATE	AMOUNT

Describe the nature of the debt and state the reason it was incurred:

_____

_____

_____

_____

_____

_____

_____

_____

STOCK OR OWNERSHIP OPTIONS

Do you have any options to purchase stock or additional ownership in the business?

YES ☐ NO ☐

If "yes":
Provide the terms of such opportunity:

OTHER

Do you have any interest in the business other than those stated above?

YES ☐ NO ☐

If "yes," describe each such interest:

_____

_____

_____

_____

_____

_____

- IDENTIFY all DOCUMENTS that show your interest in the business, money you owe the business, or money the business owes you.

- IDENTIFY each tax return filed for the business within the past four years.

- IDENTIFY each employment contract or other agreement other than a stock certificate between you and the business.

- IDENTIFY each stock restriction agreement, buy-sell agreement, or redemption agreement between you and/or your spouse and the business.

- Attach copies of all additional documents showing any interests you may have in the business identified.

DEBT WORKSHEET

Complete this worksheet for all debts, loans,* charge cards,** and other debts*** that you or your spouse owe or for which either of you is responsible.

Creditor						
Address						
Account Number						
Origination Date						
Loan Term						
Credit Limit						
Interest Rate						
Due Date						
Payment Amount						
Balance Due						

*LOANS: Including but not limited to bank loans, home equity loans, student loans, finance company loans, and personal family/friend loans.

**CHARGE CARDS: Including but not limited to credit cards (Visa, Mastercard, Discovery, American Express, etc), and department stores and gas company credit cards (Chevron, Texaco, Shell, etc.).

***OTHER DEBTS: Including but not limited to medical, legal, unpaid taxes, and debt owed to a collection agency.

INVESTMENTS

If you have the following investments, please complete all applicable sections below.

☐ Money market funds   ☐ Mutual funds
☐ Treasury bills & notes   ☐ Bonds
☐ Certificates of deposit (EE or HH savings, muni, corp, government, unit trust)

NAME (Institution/Security)		
TYPE		
ACCOUNT OR CERTIFICATE #		
DATE ACQUIRED		
ORIGINAL AMOUNT		
ORIGINAL SHARE PRICE		
INTEREST RATE		
MATURITY DATE		
FACE VALUE		
CURRENT # OF SHARES		
CURRENT TOTAL VALUE		
NAME(S) OF OWNERS		
LOCATION OF CERTIFICATE		
BROKER NAME or ACCOUNT SUPERVISOR		
BROKER PHONE NUMBER		

INVESTMENTS

If you have any of the following investments, please complete all applicable sections below.

Tax-deferred investments, including but not limited to:

☐ Keogh   ☐ 401(k)   ☐ 403(b)   ☐ Annuities   ☐ IRA

NAME (Institution/Security)		
TYPE		
ACCOUNT OR CERTIFICATE #		
DATE ACQUIRED		
ORIGINAL AMOUNT		
ORIGINAL SHARE PRICE		
INTEREST RATE		
MATURITY DATE		
FACE VALUE		
CURRENT # OF SHARES		
CURRENT TOTAL VALUE		
NAME(S) OF OWNERS		
LOCATION OF CERTIFICATE		
BROKER NAME or ACCOUNT SUPERVISOR		
BROKER PHONE NUMBER		
BENEFICIARY (IES)		
AMOUNT OF REGULAR CONTRIBUTIONS		

INVESTMENTS

If you have any of the following investments, please complete all applicable sections below.

Limited partnership, including but not limited to:

☐ Real estate   ☐ Commercial storage   ☐ Public housing
☐ Cable TV   ☐ Equipment leasing   ☐ Other

NAME (Partnership)		
TYPE		
DATE ACQUIRED		
ORIGINAL AMOUNT		
AMOUNT OF INCOME		
MONTHS INCOME RECEIVED		
AVERAGE ANNUAL TOTAL RETURN*		
CURRENT TOTAL VALUE (APPROXIMATE)		
MATURITY DATE		
NAME(S) OF OWNERS		
LOCATION OF DOCUMENT		
BROKER NAME or ACCOUNT SUPERVISOR		
BROKER PHONE NUMBER		
BENEFICIARY (IES)		

*If you receive no payments, what is value in terms of income, tax benefits, or growth?

MONTHLY EXPENSE WORKSHEET

NAME:_____ DATE:_____

EXPENSE	EXPENSE AMOUNT
Child Support	$
Alimony	
Visitation Transportation	
TOTAL SUPPORT	**$**
Rent/Mortgage	
Taxes	
Insurance	
Maintenance & Repairs	
Yard Maintenance	
Domestic Help	
Security	
Exterminator	
Storage Rental	
Association Fees	
Other (Attach list – indicate total here)	
TOTAL RESIDENCE	**$**
Gas	
Water/Refuse	
Electricity	
Telephone	
Cable	
Other (Attach list – indicate total here)	
TOTAL UTILITIES	**$**

PAGE 1: EXPENSE WORKSHEET

EXPENSE	EXPENSE AMOUNT
Furniture Payment	$
Maintenance	
Other (Attach list – indicate total here)	
TOTAL FURNITURE/APPLIANCES/ ELECTRONIC EQUIPMENT	$
Vehicle Payment	
Gasoline	
Insurance	
Maintenance & Repairs	
Parking Fares/Fees	
License	
AAA Membership	
Other (Attach list – indicate total here)	
TOTAL TRANSPORTATION/AUTO	$
Groceries/Household Supplies	
Meals Out	
School Lunches	
Other (Attach list – indicate total here)	
TOTAL GROCERY	$
Clothing – self	
Child/Children	
Laundry/Cleaning/Tailoring	
Uniforms	
Other (Attach list – indicate total here)	
TOTAL CLOTHING	$

PAGE 2: EXPENSE WORKSHEET

EXPENSE	EXPENSE AMOUNT
Medical Insurance Premium	$
Medical Uncovered – Deductible	
Dental Insurance Premium	
Dental/Orthodontia – Uncovered Premium	
Prescriptions/Supplements	
Vision Expenses – Exams/Glasses	
Chiropractor	
Other (Attach list – indicate total here)	
TOTAL MEDICAL	$
Counseling for self	
Child/Children	
Other (Attach list – indicate total here)	
TOTAL COUNSELING	$
Life/Disability Insurance – Self	
Child/Children	
Other (Attach list – indicate total here)	
TOTAL LIFE & DISABILITY INSURANCE	$
Child Expenses – Daycare	
Babysitting	
Transportation – School, Daycare	
Tuition/Tutoring/Special Needs/ College Expenses	
School – Supplies/Yearbooks/Photos/ Field Trips	
Activities – Sports/Leagues/Lessons/Camp	
Toys/Games/Hobbies/Books/Tapes/Video	
Personal Haircuts	
Other (Attach list – indicate total here)	
TOTAL CHILDCARE EXPENSES	$

PAGE 3: EXPENSE WORKSHEET

EXPENSE	EXPENSE AMOUNT
Your tuition	$
School Expenses — Books/Supplies	
Seminars/Workshops/Speakers	
Other (Attach list — indicate total here)	
YOUR TOTAL EDUCATION	$
Professional Membership Dues	
Publications	
CPA/Attorneys/Other	
Divorce Expense	
Other (Attach list — indicate total here)	
TOTAL PROFESSIONAL ACTIVITIES/EXPENSES	$
Divorce Attorney Fees	
Custody Evaluation	
Vocational/Spousal Support Evaluation	
Accountant	
Other Professionals	
Office Supplies/Copying	
Other (Attach list — indicate total here)	
TOTAL DIVORCE EXPENSES	$
Recreational Memberships (Gym, etc.)	
Hobbies/Sports	
Movies/Videos/Season Tickets	
Trips/Vacations	
Other (Attach list — Indicate total here)	
TOTAL RECREATIONAL/ ENTERTAINMENT/VACATION	$

PAGE 4: EXPENSE WORKSHEET

EXPENSE	EXPENSE AMOUNT
Savings Account	$
Retirement	
IRA	
Other (attach list – indicate total here)	
TOTAL SAVINGS/RETIREMENT/INVESTMENT	$
Church/Donations	
Subscriptions/Papers/Books/Tapes	
Gifts/Cards	
Holiday Expenses	
Personal – Manicures/Jewelry/Cosmetics	
Household Misc – Postage/ Computer/Copies	
Fees – Bank/NSF/Past Due/ Finance Charges	
Pet Expense – Grooming/Vet Food/ Pet Hotel	
Other (Attach list - indicate total here)	
TOTAL INCIDENTAL EXPENSES	$
Visa	
Mastercard	
American Express	
Discover	
Other (attach list – indicate total here)	
TOTAL CREDIT CARDS/CHARGE ACCOUNTS	$
Student Loans	
Finance Company	
Personal Loans	
Medical/Legal	
Other (attach list – indicate total here)	
TOTAL LOANS/DEBTS	$

PAGE 5: EXPENSE WORKSHEET

EXPENSE	EXPENSE AMOUNT
Back Taxes/Penalty Charges	$
Current Payment	
TOTAL TAX EXPENSES	$
Elder Parent Care	
Other (Attach list — indicate total here)	
TOTAL MISCELLANEOUS EXPENSES	$
TOTAL MONTHLY EXPENSES	$

MONTHLY INCOME WORKSHEET

NAME:_____ DATE:_____

INCOME	AMOUNT
EMPLOYMENT GROSS PAY	$
Deductions:	
Federal Withholding	
State Withholding	
FICA – Old Age	
FICA – Medicare	
Health Insurance	
Retirement	
Other (attach list – indicate total here)	
TOTAL DEDUCTIONS	$
Employment Net Pay	$
All Other Income:	
Child Support	
Alimony	
Interest/Dividends	
Net Business	
Net Rental	
Real Estate Contracts	
Trust Funds	
Retirement	
Other (attach list – indicate total here)	
TOTAL MONTHLY INCOME	$

PERSONAL BANK ACCOUNT WORKSHEET

BANK ACCOUNTS/CREDIT UNION ACCOUNTS

*Type of Account	Name & Address of Institution	Account #	Names on Account	Date Opened	Date Closed	Current Balance

Savings or Checking

CREDIT UNION ACCOUNTS

*Type of Account	Name & Address of Institution	Account #	Names on Account	Date Opened	Date Closed	Current Balance

Savings or Checking

CDs

*Type of Account	Name & Address of Institution	Account #	Names on Account	Date Opened	Date Closed	Current Balance

TRUST ACCOUNTS

*Type of Account	Name & Address of Institution	Account #	Names on Account	Date Opened	Date Closed	Current Balance

OTHER ACCOUNTS

*Type of Account	Name & Address of Institution	Account #	Names on Account	Date Opened	Date Closed	Current Balance

*Include money markets, mutual funds, ready assets, cash management accounts, etc.

REAL ESTATE WORKSHEET

Complete a worksheet for each piece of real property you or your spouse owned or had an interest in during the last three years. Attach copies of each deed, real estate contract, mortgage, lease, and option to purchase.

Address			
Location (County & State)			
Present Owner			
Purchase Price		Date of Purchase	
Down Payment		Loan No.	
Estimated Present Value:			
Annual Taxes		Annual Insurance	
FIRST MORTGAGE OR LIEN			
Balance Due $			
Owed To		Interest Rate	%
Address			
Phone		Loan No.	
TERMS			
Original Amount		Date Incurred	
Length of Loan			
Type of Instrument *(Mortgage note, real estate contract, etc.)*			
Monthly Payment Amount		Interest Rate	%
Payment Period (monthly, quarterly, etc.)			
SECOND MORTGAGE OR LIEN			
Balance Due			
Owed To			
Address			
Phone		Loan No.	
TERMS			
Original Amount		Date Incurred	
Length of Loan			
Type of Instrument *(Mortgage note, real estate contract, etc.)*			
Payment Amount		Interest Rate	%
Payment Period (monthly, quarterly, etc.)			
RENTAL PROPERTY			
Is this a rental property?			
If "yes," provide the gross rental income per month	$		

SEPARATE DEBT WORKSHEET

Description of debt:

Separate debt of (check one): ☐ Yours ☐ Your spouse

Date incurred:

Facts supporting claim:

Payments made during marriage with community funds:

Identify all documents that verify or may tend to verify the claim you have made both as to the nature of the debt and any amount of payments you claim were made during the marriage with community funds:

SEPARATE PROPERTY WORKSHEET

PROPERTY #1:

DESCRIPTION OF PROPERTY OR ASSET	
PRESENT LOCATION	
CLAIM (choose one): Separate Property, Separate Lien on Community Property, or Community Lien on Separate Property	
DATE OF ACQUISITION	
VALUE OF SOLE AND SEPARATE INTEREST	
CURRENT VALUE	
VALUE OF YOUR INTEREST ON THE DATE OF MARRIAGE	
IS THERE A DEBT AGAINST THIS PROPERTY?	☐ Yes ☐ No
DATE DEBT WAS INCURRED	
ORIGINAL BALANCE OF DEBT	
CURRENT BALANCE OF DEBT	
PAYMENT TERMS	
SOURCE OF FUNDS FOR PAYMENT	
METHOD OF COMPUTING SOLE AND SEPARATE INTEREST	

PROPERTY #2:

DESCRIPTION OF PROPERTY OR ASSET	
PRESENT LOCATION	
CLAIM (choose one): Separate Property, Separate Lien on Community Property, or Community Lien on Separate Property	
DATE OF ACQUISITION	
VALUE OF SOLE AND SEPARATE INTEREST	
CURRENT VALUE	
VALUE OF YOUR INTEREST ON THE DATE OF MARRIAGE	
IS THERE A DEBT AGAINST THIS PROPERTY?	☐ Yes ☐ No
DATE DEBT WAS INCURRED	
ORIGINAL BALANCE OF DEBT	
CURRENT BALANCE OF DEBT	
PAYMENT TERMS	
SOURCE OF FUNDS FOR PAYMENT	
METHOD OF COMPUTING SOLE AND SEPARATE INTEREST	

PROPERTY #3:

DESCRIPTION OF PROPERTY OR ASSET	
PRESENT LOCATION	
CLAIM (choose one): Separate Property, Separate Lien on Community Property, or Community Lien on Separate Property	
DATE OF ACQUISITION	
VALUE OF SOLE AND SEPARATE INTEREST	
CURRENT VALUE	
VALUE OF YOUR INTEREST ON THE DATE OF MARRIAGE	
IS THERE A DEBT AGAINST THIS PROPERTY?	☐ Yes ☐ No
DATE DEBT WAS INCURRED	
ORIGINAL BALANCE OF DEBT	
CURRENT BALANCE OF DEBT	
PAYMENT TERMS	
SOURCE OF FUNDS FOR PAYMENT	
METHOD OF COMPUTING SOLE AND SEPARATE INTEREST	

Recommended Resources

PROGRAMS

Alison Armstrong – Understanding Men

Darren Hardy – Insane Productivity

GPS Academy – School of Womanly Arts

Tony Robbins – Date with Destiny, Unleash the Power Within

BOOKS

Change Your Brain, Change Your Life by Daniel Amen

Loving the Mentally Ill by Byron Katie

Loving What Is by Byron Katie

Positive Intelligence by Shirzad Chamine

Pussy: A Reclamation by Mama Gena

The Queen's Code by Alison Armstrong

The Way of the SEAL by Mark Divine

The Work by Byron Katie (audiobook)

What Happened to You? by Bruce Perry and Oprah Winfrey

Women Who Run with the Wolves by Clarissa Pinkola Estés

Keys to the Kingdom, Alison Armstrong

Acknowledgments

First and foremost, thank you to the Mack side of my name, Terry Mack. If our marriage had been what we wanted, I would not have become the professional I am today. You taught me the best lessons in my life. I love you for that. You held the light so I could shine, even when yours was dark. Thank you to the Roybal side of my name, Deacon Eloy Roybal, Dad. Dad, you taught me that in life I would need to do hard things and could "cry all I want; just get it done."

To the best coaches on the planet, Tony Robbins and Robert Hedequist, thank you for keeping this train on the rails. Thank you to Darren Hardy for believing that I could write a book and sharing the best publishing team (Reed Bilbray, Kim Baker, Ivy Hughes, Anne Kelley Conklin, and Alyssa Rabins) with me to make this book a reality.

To Tanio McCallum, who encouraged me to share this story. To the fiery ladies who have led the way (Mama Gena, Alison Armstrong, and Marie Forleo, who reminded me why my husband hates my job).

This could not have happened without the incredible Roybal-Mack & Cordova, PC team who live to serve (Darren Cordova, Dynette Palomares, and Amelia Nelson). Special thanks to the Honorable Amber Chavez Baker, who first taught me about carrots and celery in the law library.

To the lady lawyers whose shoulders I stand on, Amy Sirignano, the late Elizabeth Whitefield, Mary Torres, and the ABA Women Rainmakers.

To close, thank you to Paul Melendres, who taught a law student how to practice law and to never take no for an answer. To save the best for last, thank you to my mother, who taught me to read and write . . . and never baked a cake. To my siblings, Emily, Reina, Nathaniel, Fran, Adam, Mary, Catherine, and Mabelle. You all carried me without expectation when times were dark and allowed me space to write this book to carry others. Finally, to the nuggets, Tanner and Lea, you are my sunshines who make me happy when skies are gray.

About the Author

Antonia Roybal-Mack is a prominent lawyer in Albuquerque, New Mexico, who has helped thousands of clients navigate divorce. Regardless of the situation her clients find themselves in—some want to leave, others are devastated that they might have to leave—Antonia leads her approach to every case with a quote from her father: "Cry all you want. Just get it done."

Antonia's "cry all you want, but get it done" attitude was influenced by her eight siblings and her parents, Deacon Eloy Roybal and Dr. Anita Roybal. Both teachers, the Roybals raised their children to value education, follow their dreams, and persist, persist, persist.

In order to maximize the benefit she provides clients, Antonia is also a master practitioner of neuro-linguistic programming (NLP), meaning she is certified to work with clients to understand how language affects their communication. As Antonia sees it, NLP means that "the words you declare become the house you live in."

Antonia has a bachelor's degree in hotel, restaurant, and tourism management from New Mexico State University and a law degree from the University of New Mexico School of Law. She is the managing partner of Roybal-Mack & Cordova Law and has received the following awards: New Mexico Business First Woman of Influence Award; the American Bar Association Law Practice Division 40 Under 40; and the New Mexico Women's Bar Association Henrietta Pettijohn Award, among others.

She has served on the Adoption Exchange Board of Directors and mentors children in the court system. She also supports hunger programs for disabled children in Belize and lobbies the government for equality for the deaf. Her daughter (a twin) was born with Down syndrome and hearing loss.

Connect with the Author

TWITTER
Antonia L. Roybal-Mack
@roybal_mack

INSTAGRAM
@Cryallyouwant_
Antonia Roybal-Mack (Personal)
Antoniaroybalmack_

LINKEDIN
Antonia Roybal-Mack (Personal)
https://www.linkedin.com/in/antonia-roybal-mack-51400183/

EMAIL
antonia@antoniaroybalmack.com
team@antoniaroybalmack.com

WEBSITE
www.roybalmacklaw.com
www.cryallyouwant.com

ROYBAL-MACK & CORDOVA, P.C.

Roybal-Mack & Cordova, P.C. provides expert legal counsel for individuals and businesses in New Mexico, specializing in family law, estate law, and personal injury. Antonia Royal-Mack founded the firm on the principle that you change society by helping one family at a time.

Our partners' roots are grounded in northern New Mexico, where advocacy on all levels is a way of life. We understand traditional New Mexico family law values and implement those as we advocate for our clients.

The firm is rooted in family law, especially helping victims of child abuse and neglect. We have developed a child- and family-centered practice that protects children and wealth at all levels. Our powerhouse of award-winning lawyers is dedicated to family advocacy.

While located in Albuquerque, New Mexico, we have a mission to protect the rights of families statewide. All of our lawyers love what they do and execute our internal motto of "work until you win."

WWW.ROYBALMACKLAW.COM

Cry All You Want. Just Get It Done.

YOUR ESSENTIAL GUIDEBOOK FOR
THRIVING THROUGH DIVORCE

Cry All You Want. Just Get It Done.

YOUR ESSENTIAL GUIDEBOOK FOR THRIVING THROUGH DIVORCE

ANTONIA ROYBAL-MACK, Esq.

LTM MEDIA GROUP, LLC

Published by LTM Media Group, LLC.

LTM | MEDIA GROUP, LLC

For ordering information or special discounts for bulk purchases, as well as to book Antonia Roybal-Mack to speak or host an event:
antoniaroybalmack.com

Cover and Interior Design by Kim Baker / Orange Brain Studio
Editing by Ivy Hughes
Copyediting by Alyssa Rabins and Anne Kelley Conklin
Proofreading by Anne Kelley Conklin
Composition by Accelerate Media Partners, LLC

ISBN 979-8-9866893-0-2

FAMILY & RELATIONSHIPS / Divorce & Separation

Printed in the United States of America

Dedication

This book is dedicated to every woman who has suffered the loss of a relationship and had to climb the mountain of divorce. Cry All You Want is for the women who have been triumphant on the other side and to those women who need to discover that "all you need is already within you now" as you tap your inner strength to simply take the next best step.

Dedication

Table of Contents

Introduction

A m I a married divorce attorney?

Yes. I am married to someone I love. Someone I have two children with and have built a life around. Someone who is bipolar, someone who has cheated on me, someone who I have left before, someone who is flawed.

WELCOME TO MARRIAGE.

I grew up in New Mexico in a staunchly Catholic household. Mom and Dad were teachers and all nine of us kids were expected to learn, grow, get an education, and excel. For me that meant making money—we never had any—so when I got to New Mexico State University, after working three jobs through undergrad and maintaining a nearly 4.0, I went into law. This wasn't an altruistic decision. I knew that there was money in law and medicine. I also knew that I didn't want to be a doctor.

There's a deeper story here, of course. After undergrad, I took a year off, partied a lot, made some poor choices, and met this wonderful man who is now 50 percent of my complicated marriage. I met Terry as I was starting the law school application process. Because I liked him, I decided to stay in New Mexico. However, if I knew then what I know now, I never would have even dated Terry. I'm convinced that the phrase "hindsight is 20/20" was created from a marriage.

One time, while I was studying for the bar exam (Terry and I were already married), he told me he had to take "some pills" every once in a while. That's all that I really knew of his mental illness. The pills were Prozac and they were being used to treat his bipolar disorder. I was young and dumb and didn't know what it meant to be bipolar. Right before the bar exam, I hacked into his email and found nude photos of a woman. It wasn't the first—or the last—time that he cheated. I left for a week; he got severely depressed and promised to change. I came back. He had no one else, and it's so ingrained in the female psyche to save the people around us, to stop the suffering, that we don't always make decisions that are in our best interest. Terry was one of those decisions, at that time.

This is where we were decades ago. Today, after having split or talked of splitting dozens of times, Terry and I still live together. However, after years of back and forth, I have put other provisions in place to protect our assets (and myself) in the event that we ever do divorce.

Throughout my fifteen-year marriage, I've experienced the back and forth of a tumultuous relationship. I've considered divorce many times. I've moved myself and my kids away from Terry, and then I've decided to stay. I've looked at what might happen to my assets if I left, and I've stayed.

I wrote *Cry All You Want* for myself. Even though I have lawyered in over a thousand divorces, when contemplating my own, I found myself scanning bookstores looking for guidance, for hope, for anything that might take away the pain of my children growing up in a one-parent household. I looked for a book with any advice on how I could protect my children while being brutally honest with myself about what needed to happen. I was desperate for something—anything—to help me deal with the fact that I was about to lose half of my law firm and engage in a momentous battle. During those times, the idea of divorce consumed all of my thoughts and energy. I thought about the separation from the time I woke up until the time that I closed my eyes, praying for sleep. Even though I knew the law, I didn't know where to turn to for support.

I imagine that you picked up *Cry All You Want* because, like me, you're at a crossroads in your marriage, confronting what *feels* like the ultimate pivot point in your life. I also imagine that what you have accomplished since the dawn of your marriage is no small feat, and that dividing it seems patently unfair. Your emotions are all over the place. You want out. The sweet smell of freedom and peace is within your grasp. But how will you move forward with work—perhaps a business—as a single woman, possibly a single mother? The questions are endless, the answers are sterile, and advice from friends has your head spinning.

I understand the psychology of what it means when women are contemplating divorce, yet when I was doing the same, I couldn't find any books that spoke to that piece of divorce and the decisions that have to be made for that to happen. But I hear from women about these challenges every day. Intelligent women who have successful careers and a successful family life come to me either seeking a divorce or devastated by the fact that their spouse is doing the same. Post-divorce, many of them thrive—however, many of them also lose their identity and really struggle to discover who they are without their marriage. They can't seem to move through the trauma of the divorce. In *Cry All You Want*, I'll show you how to be one of the women who know how to ask the right questions and make the right decisions to successfully navigate divorce and rebuild after.

Remember, your divorce is also not your mama's divorce. You are a working mother with a successful career, maybe a business. You are the one who supports the family financially. Unfortunately, even though the model of the modern family has changed, the laws have not adapted. This means that if you're contemplating divorce and you are the breadwinner, you need to read up and learn how to protect yourself. Protection, for the record, comes down to controlling your emotions, which will also protect your money.

PROTECTION, FOR THE RECORD, COMES DOWN TO CONTROLLING YOUR EMOTIONS.

As a divorce lawyer, as an almost-divorcée, and as a woman who has made it her mission to find the tools and learn the skills to navigate this entire divorce process, I will coach you on how to do just that. I will do this in the most compassionate and real way possible. In addition to having a law degree and my own firm, I have spent endless amounts of time and money to understand the language around divorce and how we use language to create frames, which creates our reality. The easiest way to understand this is in this phrase: The words you declare become the house you live in.

In my office, we've made a concerted effort to help our clients by teaching them how to communicate what they want in the throes of pain. Teaching people how to ask for what they need when they are sitting on the high road all by themselves. It is a simple concept: Intellect and emotion work inversely. If you are overwrought with emotion—even if justified—you cannot make good choices. Communication needs to pass through your emotional brain before it can get to the reasoning section of your brain.

I have almost divorced the same person numerous times. I know that, if you are facing a divorce, you feel like your financial future is uncertain. I know that you're terrified about what might happen to your kids. Even if your spouse is wonderful with them, you won't see them as much as you do now. I understand that the uncertainty devil has you staying up at night and secretly crying in the shower. I know that you secretly Google all things divorce and can't find what you're really looking for. Breathe. You have come to the right place. You have read about everything from parallel parenting and nesting to co-habitation parenting. None of it makes sense in light of those shower conversations in your head that tell you to just get it done.

This is a place where setting goals and a long-term vision for your life and your future relationships is valued. Here you will learn how to navigate these mountains of change. Here you will turn your doubt into determination.

I don't pretend for one minute that just because you're reading this, you're ready to divorce. However, there is a lot to learn from getting to the point of divorce and either going forward with it or setting different parameters around the relationship. Regardless of what you're planning to do, you have already survived every bad day in your life.

In *Cry All You Want*, we'll walk through the toughest decision you'll ever make: Should you stay or should you go? Divorce is not for everyone, no matter how intense the emotions that are driving you to consider it. So, should you stay or should you go? I'm not a fortune teller, but after decades of working with parting couples, I can provide some coaching around how to evaluate that decision. After addressing that hurdle, we'll talk about how to protect you and your children in the event that leaving is the best path forward. If you decide to stay and need some wealth protection, we will touch on that as well. Some chapters might not resonate with you. For example, chapter seven is about how to approach divorce if you're a parent, and you may not be. That's okay! Find the chapters that are most valuable to you and your situation and keep reading.

As you move through *Cry All You Want*, you'll see the bruises in my own relationship, the ones that have caused me to ask, "Should I stay or should I go?" more times than I can count. I don't hold back because I understand the complexities of navigating a relationship. You are not alone.

Cry All You Want will provide some simple answers and a lot of questions that will help move you toward or away from divorce. Remember, there are no right answers to these questions. There are only questions and results. No matter your circumstances, you will learn to own the pen that writes your story. As my dad has always told me during crisis, "Cry all you want; just get it done." The lesson is that we have to do hard things. Its okay to cry, but you still need to do the hard things.

At the end of each chapter, I'll include worksheets that will help you make the decisions that will guide your future just as I've made the ones that have guided mine. I will coach you through one of the toughest decisions that you'll ever make. The quality of the outcome depends on how honest you are with yourself about what you want. *Cry All You Want* is not about how to take your ex to the cleaners. It's about understanding your own needs and wants in a relationship (or out of it) and knowing how to go after what you most desire in this complex process.

This is like childbirth . . . painful and only you can go through it. The support on the outside does not change that only *you* can make it happen. We are women. We can walk through all pain and find beauty on the other side.

Sincerely,

"Lies don't end relationships; usually the truth does."

—SHANNON L. ALDER

www.ingramcontent.com/pod-product-compliance
Lightning Source LLC
Chambersburg PA
CBHW071950090426
42740CB00011B/1890